**W9-AQM-753**

Painting Flowers in Watercolour

Canna 'Wyoming'

Painting Flowers in Watercolour

a naturalistic approach

CORAL G. GUEST

Timber Press • Portland, Oregon

For my Mother and Father

This book owes much to the staff and students at the Royal Botanic Gardens, Kew and Dr Shirley Sherwood, whose enthusiasm has inspired me, and fostered my teaching skills over many years.

With thanks to Linda Lambert and Dorothy Moir of A & C Black, whose perceptive editing and sensitive design work has enabled the book's originality to shine through.

With thanks to Stuart, who made this book possible with his whole-hearted and practical support.

To Francis Martin for his erudite and honest advice; to Jane England and David Cousins for their generosity; to my brother and parents, Frances, Helen, Kate, Louis and Sohail, for their ongoing encouragement.

PLEASE NOTE:
In part II of the book, a grey tint appears behind some of the step-by-step illustrations. This is due to the reproduction process and does not denote that a wash should be applied.

First published in North America in 2001 by
Timber Press, Inc.
The Haseltine Building
133 S.W. Second Avenue, Suite 450
Portland, Oregon 97204, USA

ISBN 0-88192-509-8

A CIP catalog record for this book is available from the Library of Congress.

Designed by Dorothy Moir

Printed in Italy by
G. Canale & C. S.p.A. - Borgaro T.se (Turin)

Contents

PART I

PART II Flowers through the Spectrum

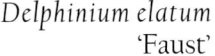

Delphinium elatum
'Faust'

Foreword

Coral Guest is amongst the very best of today's artists, fuelling the renaissance of botanical art. I love her luminous watercolours of plants, which combine meticulous observation with flowing technique and outstanding design. In this remarkable book she has managed to simplify and organise her techniques so that anyone, whatever their own level of expertise, can benefit from her wide experience and skill..

I started collecting her work in the early 1990s and have now acquired more than half a dozen paintings, one of which is the beautiful white lily shown on page 55. It has been proudly displayed with the rest of my collection all over the world, from the United States to Australia, from Sweden to South Africa and from the United Kingdom to Japan where Coral honed some of her remarkable skill with Japanese teachers.

She was one of the first artists asked to teach some of the Master Classes that I have organised over the last few years in our widely scattered Orient-Express Hotels. She has taught a couple of times in Venice and also at Reid's in Madeira. I well remember our classroom filled with earnest students practising how to do washes. Suddenly Coral cried out, 'Don't forget to breathe!' It is the human element of her teaching, her patient, charming and generous personality that comes across, not only in the classroom but also in this book.

She has gone into the greatest detail here and shows how to avoid many of the pitfalls that can occur with equipment and transient plant materials. It has been very difficult to obtain basic technical knowledge of watercolour techniques in art schools recently, so many students emerge without even knowing how to tackle a wash or compose a plant portrait. They will find that Coral's wide teaching experience and great artistic ability have combined to create something really useful and stimulating. She has illustrated it with her own naturalistic flower portraits, setting the highest standards for her readers and making it an attractive book to browse through as well as a teaching manual. I am sure it will be an inspiration for others, whether beginners or experienced artists.

Dr Shirley Sherwood
1 August 2000

Camellia japonica 'Adolphe Audusson'

Strelitzia reginae

Introduction

Naturalistic Flower Painting portrays natural beauty in natural light, using traditional watercolour techniques to convey the vibrant colour and delicate textures of the plant world. This book provides practical working methods for painting plants in this naturalistic style, with the emphasis upon the development of observational skills through different areas of study. As a creative process, it offers the means to achieve a faithful representation of a flower.

Realism and truth to nature are the guiding principles of the naturalistic approach to flower painting, and an historical perspective reveals the beginnings of this art in the flower borders of the medieval manuscripts of Flanders and Burgundy. In these miniature works, opaque watercolour was used for the creation of realistic flower images existing in world of natural light and shade. Many individual European artists of the 16th and 17th centuries developed this particular modus operandi by producing larger watercolours that were entirely devoted to flowers, with no reference to other secular or religious subjects. For the earlier artist the flora played a supporting role as part of a composite scene. For the artists of a later generation, the flower itself became the focus of a lifetime's work.

A system of patronage allowed these artists to flourish and develop their skills producing highly specialised works of art, painted in a naturalistic style. Global exploration and the opening of trade routes brought new species of plants to Western Europe, and the collectors of flower paintings were in many cases the owners of these valuable and unusual plants. Artists such as Dürer, Jacopo Ligozzi, Georg Flegel and many more known and anonymous painters were engaged in portraying common garden plants as well as flowers that were, at the time, prized for their rarity.

Various techniques were employed, ranging from transparent watercolour to gouache, onto surfaces as diverse as vellum, paper and ivory. This was a painting style that depicted fine details, creating virtuoso works that were designed to be seen close-up, rather than from a distance. Many groups of themed pictures were stored in folios and placed in libraries, as most works of this kind were exclusively for private viewing, and not meant for exhibition. For the Renaissance flower painter, observable truth was synonymous with beauty, and their studies of flowering plants were intended as works of art in their own right. The linear drawings created for the early herbals, produced to assist plant identification, appear in marked contrast to these realistic images.

During the 18th and 19th centuries, naturalistic flower painting almost disappeared into obscurity as the watercolour medium was absorbed into the realms of botanical illustration, and art endeavoured to serve science and horticulture. From the beginning of the 20th century, the flower piece as a work of art remained largely in the hands of accomplished amateurs and went more or less publicly unrecognised. The finest examples of historic Naturalism to be found in England are stored in the archives of the Royal Botanic Gardens, Kew, the Royal Horticultural Society Lindley Library, the British Museum, the Victoria & Albert Museum, and the Broughton Collection at the Fitzwilliam Museum in Cambridge.

In the early 1970s, flower painting began a new chapter in its history with the work of the late Rory McEwen, and today it continues to receive attention from both artists and collectors. This is reflected in the number of galleries now showing works by individual artists, such as Raymond C. Booth, Paul Jones and Elizabeth Blackadder, whose work has entered the mainstream of art. The training of flower painters and botanical illustrators has traditionally fallen under the auspices of botanical and horticultural institutions, as opposed to art schools. In the mid-1980s, under the guidance of Dr. Brinsley Burbidge, Laura Giuffrida and Gren Lucas, the Royal Botanic Gardens, Kew, began to offer Flower Painting tuition alongside their Botanical Illustration courses and to stage exhibitions of contemporary botanical art at the Kew Gardens Gallery. The Royal Horticultural Society in London includes Botanical Art as part of its autumn and winter flower shows in the Westminster Halls, and the Hunt Institute for Botanical Documentation, Carnegie-Mellon University, Pittsburgh, USA, holds large biannual exhibitions of work by contemporary artists. Much of the raising of public interest in the genre is a result of the significant contribution of energy and endeavour made by Dr. Shirley Sherwood, whose renowned collection of Contemporary Botanical Art has travelled the globe in a series of large-scale exhibitions that have consistently received record attendances. In 1996, Dr. Sherwood established the worldwide series of Master Classes, which continues to inspire an increasing number of artists to paint plants.

This book is a response to the many requests that I have received for teaching, and which owing to the demands of flower painting, I am unable to provide.

Part I describes the specific techniques that are essential to the creation of the colour and texture of petals and other plant surfaces. It emphasises the importance of observational drawing as a foundation for painting. The purist method of working with transparent watercolour, which utilises the whiteness of the paper to achieve highlights and pale tints, is explained in detail. In addition, Part I deals with different methods of preliminary work, which facilitates the move forward to the production of a more highly finished painting.

Part II of the book is devoted to the observation of individual flowers in a systematic procedure, applying the methods and techniques described in Part I. The plants included are structurally varied. Therefore, some are simple to execute and others are.a little more challenging. Each specimen flower is characterised as an individual plant, painted life-size, and observed in isolation. Specific issues, such as the highlight on leaves and various surface textures, are analysed as they occur. Plants in this section have an inflorescence of a distinct colour. These provide a focus for painting the various colour rays of the visible spectrum, and each individual flower reveals a variety of tints and shades within that ray. The colour green is not included as a specific flower colour because this not a regular occurrence. However, green is analysed in its diversity throughout the buds, leaves and stems of some of the individual plants, and the mixing of greens receives specific attention in Part I.

The methods described in this handbook are academic in origin, and biased toward the needs of the flower painter. These are intended to be of use to artists on all levels, from the absolute beginner to the serious amateur and professional artist wishing to turn their skills to flower painting.

The text uses some botanical terms as well as the botanical names of plants. These terms and descriptions support the development of accurate observational skills, and give due respect to the identity of each plant. As a practical measure, botanical terms replace lengthy and wordy explanations. A glossary of these terms is located towards the end of the book. A Selected Bibliography is also included, to suggest further reading on a variety of subjects relating to the flower painter's art. Finally, a Suppliers Directory provides easy access to the materials and equipment recommended in this book.

This handbook is for all those who seek to express a love of the natural world through the painting of flowers. A picture is often said to be complete when any further additions will lead to confusion rather than clarity. Therefore, what we exclude from a picture holds as much significance as what we choose to include. As a creative process, the painting of flowers serves to nurture this capacity for artistic discernment, but above all else it is the genuine appreciation of flowers and the joy felt in their presence, that brings this art into being.

1 Equipment

Drawing board and clips

Artists' drawing boards of all sizes are available from art suppliers. Choose one which is no less than 5mm (^{1}/4 in) thick, to ensure that it does not warp. An A2 size (420mm x 594mm / 16^1/2 in x 23^7/16 in) plywood drawing board was used for the work in this book. A drawing board can be homemade from 5mm (^{1}/4 in) thick plywood, which requires sanding and sealing with a protective layer of clear varnish.

Other suitable materials for a drawing board are medium density fibreboard (MDF) and melamine coated chipboard. It is useful to build a collection of several drawing boards with differing dimensions, for various sizes of paper. To attach the paper to the drawing board use metal drawing board clips that slip over the board and paper, or bulldog clips. Blu-Tack, masking tape or drawing pins are not suitable as they the mark the paper.

Easel and drawing board tables

The drawing board requires an easel of some kind, and there are many styles on the market. The best option is always the one that feels the most comfortable to use. The traditional preference for a painter is an upright, free standing, hardwood easel. Its solid perpendicular form allows the best possible view of a picture. These are available in a range of woods and styles from art shops and mail order catalogues. This type of easel was utilised for work featured in this book.

An adjustable tabletop easel is a suitable alternative to a free standing easel. A drawing board table consisting of an adjustable drawing board that is built into a table is another option. This type is favoured by designers and illustrators, and it is available from graphic art shops. A drawing board on a stand is a similar solution. This has legs and an adjustable support for the board, but no table. If you do not plan to invest in this expensive piece of equipment, it is perfectly possible to work on a board that is leant against a pile of telephone books placed on a table top.

Tables

When using an upright easel, or drawing board stand, two small tables are also required - one for the plant and the other for the palette, paints etc. These positions can be easily readjusted if the tables are on casters. If you are using a table easel, the plant and palettes should be positioned either side of you on the table area. Refer to Chapter 5 for details on setting up equipment in the workspace.

Chair

A comfortable, upright, and supportive chair is preferable to a stool. Choose one that is an appropriate height for working at the easel or table.

Vase

For cut flowers, use a glass vase, or dish, that is appropriate for the size of the plant.

Water jars

Use two generous water jars made of clear glass: one to provide clean water for mixing colours, and the other for cleaning brushes.

Palettes

The palette must be white to facilitate accurate colour assessment. Manufacturers produce white palettes in a range of shapes and sizes, and, from a variety of materials, such as ceramic, plastic and enamel. Ceramic is the best option, because water-colour will not stain it. A stack of small, flat, white, china tea plates will provide an endless supply of clean palettes. When painting, reserve one for reds, one for greens, one for blues etc. This ensures that the colours remain clean and bright. When a palette appears too crowded, take a clean plate and continue mixing. To save time, wash all the plates at the end of the painting session.

BRUSHES

It is worth investing in good quality watercolour brushes. Although expensive, they will retain their shape when loaded with paint, and last well. The sable brush is unequalled in its ability to glide a smooth wash onto paper and produce a precise point. Brushes made from a mixture of prolene and sable can be useful for sketching work. Brushes made entirely from synthetic hairs (suitable for vegetarians and vegans), squirrel or ox hair, all fail to respond as well as sable.

Brushes labelled Artist's Sable or Pure Sable range from the excellent to the good, depending on the quality of the hair. Sable itself varies in quality, but the Kolinsky sable is without doubt the premium grade. All major producers of art materials such as Winsor & Newton and Rowney manufacture their own Kolinsky sable brushes. Other brands such as da Vinci and Raphael are available from larger art centres. Each company produces several numbered series of sable brushes in a range of different qualities, lengths and sizes. Choose medium length round brushes that are able to hold sufficient paint whilst maintaining a fine point. Flat brushes are not used. Prices vary considerably, with the very finest quality Kolinsky sables, such as Raphael Series 8404, and the Winsor and Newton Series 7, costing as much as three times the price of an average good quality Kolinsky sable. These top of the range brushes are a worthwhile investment, and have the longest life of all the sable brushes. For the paintings featured in this book, the widely available, average good quality Rowney Kolinsky Sable Series 40 was used.

All brushes are numbered to denote their size, beginning with the lowest number for the thinnest brush. The four main sizes required for Flower Painting are:
N° 1 for detailed work

N° 3 for small areas of wash and for detail
N° 5 for general areas of wash, and some detail
N° 6 for large areas of wash

There are no precise standards for the manufacturing of brush sizes. Consequently, the same numbered sizes may vary moderately from brand to brand. The very finest brushes are made to a slightly larger specification than those that are less costly.

After use, wash brushes carefully with a bar of hand soap and lukewarm water, then rinse them thoroughly. The best type of soap is vegetable or olive oil soap, containing no lanolin or perfume. Avoid liquid detergents made for clothes and crockery, as these contain strong cleaning agents that hasten the breakdown of the delicate hairs. Use an absorbent cloth or kitchen towel to dry the brushes, then reshape and repoint them with the finger tips whilst they are damp. Never put a wet brush in the mouth to repoint it, as small particles of paint may prove toxic if taken internally. Store the brushes flat, and keep them free from dust.

RULERS

Two transparent plastic rulers will assist accurate plant drawing. A long ruler, approximately 40cm (16in) in length, and a short ruler, approximately 15cm(6in) in length, are the most useful.

PLUMB LINE

A plumb line is comprised of a metal weight, which is fixed to a length of thread or line. This is used in drawing work to test a true perpendicular. These are available from art stores and builder's merchants, or made by tying strong thread around the lid of a tube of paint.

STUDIO SPACE, LIGHT FITTINGS & LIGHT BULBS

Refer to Chapter 5 for specific details of setting up the workspace and to the Suppliers Directory for lighting equipment.

BOTANICAL BOOKS

Some basic understanding of the subject will provide support when working on plant drawings. Refer to the Selected Bibliography for suggested titles.

2 Materials

PAPER

Good quality watercolour paper made from 100% acid free cotton rag is essential. Flower painting techniques demand a watercolour paper with a smooth Hot-Pressed surface (often termed HP, and sometimes called Satinata). This is vellum's modern equivalent.

This paper is usually pressed when hot, between large metal sheets. This process, which renders it smooth, is known as calendering. Glue size is applied during the manufacturing process. This prevents the watercolour from 'bleeding' and allows clear brush marks to be painted onto the surface.

Most art shops stock paper from various manufacturers, such as Fabriano, Aquarelle Arches, Saunders Waterford, Winsor & Newton, and Lana. This is all mould-made paper, produced in paper mills and widely available. It normally has two deckle edges and two straight edges. For the preliminary work in Part I, and the pictures that are documented in Part II, Fabriano Artistico 600gsm Hot Pressed (Satinata) watercolour paper was used. A 300gsm Hot-Pressed acid free paper from any well-known brand is equally suitable. The very finest papers, such as Twinrocker, are hand-made, produced from 100% cotton, and have four deckle edges.

The dimensions of a sheet of mould-made paper are approximately 560 x 760mm / 22 x 30in. This can be cut into smaller sheets when necessary. Papers display subtle differences in their degree of 'whiteness'. It is always advisable to experiment with paper from different manufacturers to find the one that suits you best. The heaviness, or thickness, of paper is gauged metrically per square metre or imperially per ream.

There are three main grades of paper weight:

180gsm (metric)/90lb (imperial) the thinnest paper.
300gsm (metric)/140lb (imperial) the medium thickness paper.
600gsm (metric)/300lb (imperial) the thickest paper.

The 180gsm paper will cockle and warp when wet, and requires 'stretching' onto a board before use, to ensure that it dries flat. The stretching method involves wetting a sheet of paper and fixing its edges to a board with brown paper gum strip. When the paper is dry, it is 'stretched', and ready for use. The use of a heavier paper of 300gsm or 600gsm weight circumvents the need for stretching. The 300gsm paper heaves slightly when wet, but dries flat. This widely used and easily available paper has substance and durability. There is a difference in cost between the light, medium and heavy weight papers. The extra cost of the medium or heavy weight paper is moderately offset by the need to purchase gummed tape for stretching the lighter papers.

The 600gsm paper does not move at all when wet, and is consequently the most expensive, but it provides a solid, enduring, and substantial surface on which to paint. The larger, more comprehensive art suppliers stock the 600gsm paper. You can access these through searching the classified sections of art magazines, or online art stores.

Either side of the paper can be used for painting, because both sides are sized. Even so, the paper does have a specific front and back. To determine this, observe that on the front of the paper the deckle edge is flush with the paper surface, which has a fine grain, rather like blotting paper. On the back of the paper, there is a step down to the deckle edge. The back surface has an extremely feint mesh-like imprint upon it that comes from the base of the papermaking bed. The placement of a watermark differs with each brand name, and manufacturers will sometimes change the position of a watermark. It is therefore a not entirely reliable means of testing for the front or back.

For sketching and study work in watercolour, use sheets or large blocks of watercolour paper that are cut to the required size. For Thumbnail Sketches (see Chapter 15), use cartridge or graph paper, or a block of thin layout paper. In addition, blotting paper size 130 x 250mm (5x10in.) should be placed beneath the painting hand to keep the watercolour paper clean and free from hand grease.

WATERCOLOUR PAINT
See Chapter 9 for the recommended range of colours.

Watercolour paint differs from brand to brand. Some have a stiff consistency and others are more gluey. Above all, it is preferable to use Artists' Quality Watercolour Paint. This is the finest quality because there is a high ratio of pigment contained in the paint. It is also more finely ground than the student quality and easier to work with. The colours also possess greater permanence. It is perfectly acceptable to mix colours from different manufacturers. Well-known brand names include Da Vinci, Winsor & Newton, Old Holland (not to be confused with the Rembrandt brand), Sennelier, Lucas, and Rowney. Colours may alter slightly from brand to brand. For the sake of consistency Winsor and Newton Artist's Watercolour has been used throughout for the samples in this book.

Watercolour paint comes in the form of tubes or blocks (traditionally known as pans). Tubes generally come in three sizes of 14 ml (0.47 US fl oz), 7.5ml and 5ml, depending on the brand. Pans come simply in half-pans or pans. A little watercolour paint goes a long way, and the smaller quantities are appropriate for flower painting unless you wish to produce very large pieces of work. To categorise the price, all paint is labelled with a series number. Tubes facilitate a freer, more rapid style of colour mixing, owing to their fluid consistency. They are extremely easy to mix on the palette, and richness and depth of colour are easily obtained. Pans are semi-moist to dry,

depending on the colour. These require water to soften the block and make the colour ready for use. Pans can encourage a restrictive approach to painting, and it can be time consuming to transfer paint from the paint box to the palette for colour mixing. However, pans do not create wasted paint, as tubes may easily do. Tube colour was used for all of the paintings in this book, but the choice of either tubes or pans remains a personal one.

PENCILS
A pencil lead is a graphite compound that varies in hardness. The HB and H grades are required for flower painting. The HB is a medium grade that produces a point that wears down quite quickly with use. It is suitable for sketching on drawing, cartridge, and watercolour paper, and is useful for writing notes. The H is a hard grade that produces a fine point. It is suitable for accurate drawing onto cartridge and watercolour paper.

ERASER
A kneadable putty eraser is more effective than the hard plastic type. This will not damage the surface of the paper or leave behind small fragments and particles.

PAINT RAGS
Use kitchen paper to soak up surplus paint or water from the paintbrush.

FLORIST'S FOAM
This is sold under several brand names and widely available as 'Oasis'. This is used to support flower stems.

KNIFE AND SCALPEL
A craft knife is suitable for sharpening pencils to a fine point. A scalpel with disposable blades is ideal for cutting plant material. Both are available from art stores. Remove all blades when not in use and place well away from small children.

1 Iris germanica

3 Plant Material

POT GROWN PLANTS

The supply of fresh and healthy plant material is an ongoing concern for the flower painter. Many flowers that do not survive well as cut flowers, thrive well when cultivated in pots, providing that the soil and weather conditions are suitable. Pot grown plants from nurseries and florists are widely available, and are a vast source of subject matter for the flower painter.

Generally, it is best to grow each plant individually in its own pot so it can be easily moved into the studio. If the stem of a pot grown plant is to be portrayed with a cut end, as in Figure 12, it is preferable to delay this cutting until the painting is almost finished. Attach the stem to a cane that is placed beside it in the pot, to keep it in place after it is cut.

Pot grown flowers, and larger container grown herbaceous plants and flowering shrubs, can be cultivated in the garden or glasshouse, or acquired directly from a nursery at flowering time. A terrace, a patio, a balcony or even a window ledge can provide good growing conditions for the right plant. Many beautiful houseplants flower comfortably in the home, are easy to maintain, and provide worthwhile subject matter.

National horticultural shows regularly include exhibitions from specialist growers who display plants in pots and large containers. Expert growers will assist you in supplying information about a plant, its availability, and its maintenance. You can access specialist growers through websites, horticultural publications and magazines. (See Suppliers Directory.)

CUT FLOWERS

It is perhaps no coincidence that many great flower painters of the past have been passionate gardeners. A garden that grows flowers specifically for cutting is a wonderful asset and a superb source of flowers for an artist. A well-managed cutting garden can provide subjects for painting throughout the year. This is by far the most labour intensive way to acquire cut flowers, but for anyone who loves to garden there are no disadvantages.

If you have a small outdoor space or balcony, flowers can be grown closely together in grow-bags or pots, until ready for cutting. Gardeners exhibiting cut flowers at horticultural shows are often willing to part with their carefully tended cultivars at the end of a show. If you live in the heart of the city and have no access to a garden, or you do not have time to grow plants, access to a good florist is essential. A discerning florist can provide an invaluable service by offering a continuous supply of fresh flowers. Take your custom to one who is willing to obtain a wide range of high quality plants and has a good knowledge of what is in season.

Most major cities have wholesale flower markets that stock a huge variety of flowers from commercial growers across the globe. Florists obtain flowers from these markets, which open for trade in the early hours of the morning. Although wholesale, many such markets are open to the public. Prices are lower, but bulk purchases are sometimes necessary, unless it is late in the trading day and odd boxes of flowers remain unsold. In addition to the wholesale markets, individual European florist shops receive deliveries from fleets of refrigerated vans, containing vast quantities of cut flowers in bud, from the commercial growers in The Netherlands.

PLANT MAINTENANCE

Many plants are not too disturbed during the day when placed in a room with sufficient natural light. The heat of an electric light can pose a problem, sometimes causing a plant to distort or open prematurely. Therefore, when using a lamp, ensure that there is enough ventilation in the room, and take a break from the painting when the plant shows signs of overheating. During a break, turn off the lamp and face it away from the plant. Spray the plant with a fine water mist if necessary.

Return a potted plant to the outdoors or glasshouse after each painting session, to ensure that its normal growth patterns are disturbed as little as possible. A plant that lives outside should not remain in the studio over night.

Cut flowers are best left in their water containers and placed in a fridge during the night. This provides a cool temperature, moist air and darkness. These conditions tend to slow down the rate of a flower's growth into bloom, and many cut flowers can be stored for a few days in this way without damage to their development. To ensure that any delicate plant matter will not freeze, the fridge should not be set at a very low temperature. Never attempt to freeze flowers because they break down rapidly as they thaw. Many cut flowers benefit from being enclosed in a roomy cellophane bag (the sort used by florists to wrap bouquets), before being placed in the refrigerator.

Flowers with developed buds will burst into bloom very quickly when taken from a cool fridge into a warm room. Acclimatise them slowly, by placing them in a cool shaded room for about an hour, before taking them into the studio. The *Iris germanica*, Figure 1 on page 15, was acclimatised in this way, to prevent the flower buds from opening too quickly.

A so-called Dewpoint Cabinet, the kind used by florists to keep orchids, is an expensive but fine addition to any flower painter's studio. Such cabinets have clear glass doors and walls that allow natural light to reach the plant. They also have electric lighting, plus temperature and moisture controls. (For suppliers see Suppliers Directory.)

Flowers that move during a painting session can sometimes be problematic, particularly flowers with fleshy stalks, such as *Tulipa* cultivars, which quickly turn their heads towards the light. Buy these when they are still in bud and give them time to adjust before choosing which ones to paint. Some *Paeonia* cultivars that drop their petals when cut will tolerate having tailor's pins fixed through the base of their petals and into the top of their stems. If done with care, this can prevent a petal from falling just long enough for that part of the painting to be completed. A 1cm ($^{1}/2$ in) width strip of clear cellophane, wrapped around a closed flower or bud, will also stop a bud from opening. Cut the strip, wrap it securely but carefully around the bud or flower, and hold it together with clear sticky tape. It is not necessary or advisable to use these remedies on a regular basis, but only as a last resort.

Various strategies will sustain flowers and encourage stems to drink after cutting. Most stems absorb more water when cut at an oblique angle, rather than straight across. Florists recommend splitting fibrous and woody stems to a length of approximately 3cm ($1^{1}/4$ in). You can revive delicate cut flowers by pouring warm water into their container. Change the water for cut flowers every day without fail. Cut flower food is beneficial at all times for florist's flowers, and some profess that lemonade and aspirin are useful stimulants. If you have some concern about a specific plant, consult the nurseryman or florist who supplied it.

CONTAINERS FOR FLOWERS AND CUTTINGS

Choose a solid clear glass vase, or jar, for cut flowers, so that the water level is visible. Florist's foam (generally sold under the brand name 'Oasis') is useful for positioning flower stems and cuttings from flowering shrubs and trees. The size of the container should reflect the size of the plant, providing a plentiful supply of water and a roomy space for the stems.

If the stems of the flowers are to be painted, only raise the water level in the vase to a height of 3-5cm (1-2in.), to prevent stems and leaves from rotting down too quickly. Remember to top up the water supply at regular intervals. Flower stems will appear distorted if viewed through curved glass, so remember to remove them from their vase before drawing or painting. Reposition them in Oasis foam, or a wire armoire, placed securely in a shallow but solid dish, containing water. To support small cuttings, small flowers or flower heads with short stalks, use a block of wet Oasis foam on a saucer or small dish. To give stable and secure height to small flowers, secure a block of Oasis foam into the top of a jar filled with water, and place the small flowers into the top surface of the foam. For the observation of the cut end of a stem, a straight stem may be removed from the foam support and secured with masking tape to the outside of a straight-sided vase. Keep the stem in a position that accords with the painting.

PLANT CHARACTERISTICS

The flowering of an individual plant bears a direct relationship to its environment. Species growing in their natural habitat have evolved by adapting to soil and weather conditions, and the surrounding plant and animal life. The hybridisation of plants by commercial growers has made a huge range of plants available to the gardener and florist, resulting in plants with extended flowering seasons, larger blooms and many colour variations.

Every type of plant requires a set of suitable conditions to enable it to fulfil its life cycle. Some plants can tolerate modifications in weather and soil and still flourish. Nevertheless, a plant may alter or vary its typical appearance if its regular or indigenous environment changes. Many plants from remote regions of the world will grow well in a domestic garden, but in so doing, may exhibit subtly different characteristics to those displayed in their place of origin. The blooms from common garden plants, such as continuous flowering hybrid tea roses, and cultivars of red *Camellia japonica* will alter their colour very subtly when a change of weather occurs. The roses blooming in full sun, at the height of an English summer, appear slightly paler in colour than those from the same plant that come into bloom during dull grey days of late September. Red *Camellia japonica* blooms need a shady position and will be bleached by the sun if left in a south facing part of the garden.

Forced flowers that are cultivated commercially under artificial lighting conditions may express a similar change in appearance. This is sometimes dramatic in the richer coloured flowers, such as the purple *Eustoma*, where artificial glasshouse light bleaches pigmentation to such a degree that the overlapped petals which have received less light, are a deeper colour.

Soil pH balance can also affect the colour of flowers. An obvious example is the ubiquitous mop-head *Hydrangea*, which develops reddish-pink coloured blooms when grown on alkaline soils, but produces blue coloured blooms when grown in the presence of aluminium salts or iron.

A naturalistic flower painting is a visual record based on observation, and understanding any effects that environmental changes have on the plant is relevant to the realism of the work. It is always appropriate to chronicle these facts, by recording the source of a plant and the growing conditions, by notating any sketching or study work, and by keeping notebooks for future reference. Finished works benefit from having these details written in pencil on the reverse of the paper.

2 *Camellia japonica* 'Adolphe Audusson' colour study

Camellia japonica

'Adolphe Audusson'

4 Work in Progress

USING THIS HANDBOOK

For those new to watercolour painting, it is necessary to practise the wash techniques before attempting to paint a whole flower. Paint the washes onto a sheet of paper, following the procedures in Chapter 7. Keeping each experiment to approximately the same size as those in this book and using the same size brush as in the sample, repeat each wash several times over until you feel comfortable with the process. Thereafter, experiment with mixing the neutral tint mixture, described in Chapter 11, and follow this with a copy of the Tint and Shade scale described in Chapter 12. When you have acquired a plant subject, you will need to apply the preliminary work procedures (see pages 57-68) before working on a finished painting. This working process includes the Thumbnail Sketch, the Tonal Sketch and Colour Study, which provide the opportunity to experiment with washes and dry brush techniques. Beginners in particular will find these methods useful for learning how to combine techniques to suit a particular plant subject.

Ensure that you feel happy about your choice of plant before you begin to paint. Part II includes a variety of possible plant subjects, some are intricate and others are less so. The *Anemone*, *Tulipa* and *Canna* cultivars are all suitable subjects for beginners, and it is also useful for beginners to paint a small part of a more complex plant, such as a small section of a *Delphinium*, showing one or two florets. For artists on an intermediate level, the previous three plants as well as the *Strelitzia reginae*, the *Fritillaria imperialis*, and the *Camellia japonica* are all worthy subjects. All of the plants recommended in Part II are appropriate for painters with more experience, but the *Lilium longiflorum* and the *Delphinium* are the most challenging. If you are unable to acquire any of these plants, obtain one from the same genus, that has a similar colour and form, and adapt and apply the suggestions in this book, in accordance with your own observation.

CHOOSING A PLANT AND A PROJECT

Beyond the recommendations and examples in this book, there is a vast range of flora from which to choose. Always select a plant that brings you joy, inspires your creativity and offers you the appropriate artistic challenges. Encourage yourself to progress, and guide your own improvements by taking an objective view of your abilities. Work within your limitations, but continue to extend the boundaries further and further, so that your skills develop. Do not restrict yourself by repeating what you have done well, simply out of fear of failure.

Always be generous to yourself by acknowledging the achievements that you have made, whilst being truthful with yourself about what requires more work. As mistakes are natural, seeing them as a learning curve is the best approach to take. If a painting fails, try to understand why it did so, evaluate its usefulness in terms of experience, and give yourself time to assimilate what you have learnt.

When you are confident with these techniques and wish to expand your range of subjects, do so with an open mind. Some plants will appeal to you more than others. However, choosing a wide range of subjects will help your work to progress and develop. For this reason, it is wise to take an honest look at your work. There maybe things that you find particularly difficult to paint. This may be certain aspects of flowers, such as the highlights on leaves, the transparency of petals, fine details, etc. Choosing a subject that ensures these problems are tackled will benefit both your work and your confidence in the long term. If you have difficulty with one of the working methods described in this book, such as drawing, or the tonal sketch, it will be useful for you to spend more time on these subjects. If, for example, you find both tone and the depiction of highlights on leaves problematic, it would be a useful exercise to combine these two issues by painting glossy leaves in monochrome.

If you are an absolute beginner, choose a flower with a single stem and relatively few petals. Plants that display simple flowers or a single row of petals are good subjects for practising basic drawing and watercolour techniques. A plant that is not overly complex will take relatively little time to paint and enable you to develop techniques without the distraction of a difficult plant structure. At this initial stage, avoid flowers that are very large, or ones that are extremely small. Whole flower spikes or flower heads composed of an intricate arrangement of florets, may also pose too many problems during this stage. Progress forward to these more complex plants when you have completed several pictures of less difficult subjects.

It is a worthwhile exercise for all artists to paint the same flower several times. This may seem an archaic means of learning, but it does promote fast learning. This discipline creates the opportunity to clearly observe strengths and weaknesses and refine working methods.

Plants that flower continuously through the summer months, or those that have a long flowering season, such as herbaceous perennials and various species of houseplant, are all good subjects for this kind of project. In addition, many florists' flowers such as lilies, irises and carnations are available continuously over a long season.

For this type of project, work repeatedly for as little as half an hour each day, over a month or two, using the methods described in this book. Produce sketches, studies and small finished paintings of the plant at various stages of growth. Set an overall time limit for the project and set aside regular times to paint, if this is practicable. When the task is complete, compare all the work produced during the assignment and assess your improvements.

A collection of themed pictures works well as a focus for artistic development, particularly if you have reached an intermediate or advanced stage and are in search of a goal. After some experience, most flower painters will give their attention to the plants that they find the most interesting. Most professional flower painters have clear preferences for a particular family of plants and tend to build up a body of work that explores those concerns. Themes can vary considerably, and the options are limitless. The most popular theme is a choice of flowering plants from one genus, which has occupied some artists for many years. Other themes can be less time-consuming and more idiosyncratic, such as flowers from bulbs; herbaceous perennials; old-fashioned roses; spring-flowering trees; bog plants; or wild flowers from a particular region or country.

If you intend to paint flowers from species that belong to a particular region, do remember that it is not good practice to pick or uproot plants from the wild, even if their conservation status will allow this. Many indigenous flower seeds, and rare species of plants from around the globe, are now commercially grown. If you have a particular desire to paint a plant that you cannot procure for yourself, the best option is to make studies in the field, once you have obtained any necessary permission to enter the plant's habitat.

FORWARD PLANNING
It is of no benefit to work from memory or imagination and to 'fill-in' any unfinished parts of a painting in this way is a pointless exercise. With complex, large or short-lived plants, it may be possible to paint only some aspects of a plant during one flowering season. The work can be resumed the following year, but it is necessary to keep research notes on the precise flowering time of the plant to enable you to obtain the right specimens and set aside time for the completion of the work.

For organising a constant supply of plants, and for long-term projects that are devoted to a theme, a year planner and a pocket diary are indispensable items. Use them to plan the growing and cutting of flowers at home, and the ordering and collection of flowers from nurseries, florists and other sources. Alongside this, coordinate the time that you have available to paint, and include any plans for commissioned work and dates for your exhibitions.

If you are growing plants yourself, it is always advisable to extend the flowering season for as long as possible, and to cultivate plants to flower in succession. This ensures a plentiful supply of plants, as well as allowing for some flexibility in your arrangements for painting time. A prolonged supply of flowers, either homegrown, or from a florist or nursery, offers you more time to observe a plant's typical characteristics. The bulbs for the blooms in the painting of *Tulipa* 'Gudoshnik', Figure 3, were planted in succession to allow for the completion of a series of sketches and studies, as well as a large painting of flowers at various stages of growth.

As flowers grow and decay, their colouring may alter dramatically. Most flowers find their optimum level of brilliance during their peak flowering time, and then fade, revert to green, deepen in colour, or go brown, before breaking down. It is useful to have enough time and plant material to allow for these observations, before starting to paint or draw. *Camellia japonica* 'Adolphe Audusson', Figure 2, is a Colour Study painted from a large container grown plant. This flowered over several weeks, allowing enough time for many sketches and studies to be painted, before the finished work (documented in Part II) was completed.

TIME

For the flower painter, time is of the essence, and efficient planning and effective plant maintenance can overcome many problems that the lack of time imposes.

The issue of working with comparatively short-lived plant matter has to be weighed against the amount of time that is available in which to paint. This may lead the artist to feel a certain pressure that, for some, is not conducive to a precise manner of painting. If you are a beginner or if you naturally paint very slowly, these difficulties can be overcome through an appropriate choice of plant. Plants that are long lasting, or with a simple inflorescence, as well as small parts of

more complex plants, are options that will alleviate these pressures. Flowers generally have a shorter life than leaves, and it is often necessary to paint those first when working on a highly finished piece of work, such as the ones featured in Part II of this book.

It is normal for beginners to spend more time than necessary on mixing colours or to find that they have not mixed enough paint. With time and practice, a fluent coordination is achievable as one becomes more comfortable with the medium. The length of time taken to complete a picture is different for each individual artist and the amount of time devoted to painting work is a personal choice. Some artists will work at a fast and optimum level for only a few hours in the day, and others will accomplish the same amount of work by painting slowly and methodically from dawn until dusk. Experienced professional painters all work at differing speeds, some spending weeks on one small plant and others only a few days. For this reason, a precise record of the amount of time taken to complete each picture featured in Part II is not included. All flower painters are limited by the life span of their flower subjects, and we must consider this and the time we have available, before choosing a plant to paint.

3 Tulipa 'Gudoshnik'

5 The Workspace

THE ROOM

The ideal studio space has ample light from a north-facing window, and sufficient space to place the equipment and store materials and paintings. A room of this description is an advantage but not a necessity, as any room that has sufficient space to accommodate the basic equipment is suitable for use as a studio. A dining room or study is the easiest room to adapt, where a studio may be set up using the existing furniture, such as a chair, table and desk. If the plant appears to merge with the background of furniture and objects, it is useful to place a piece of white paper or card behind the plant or to cover the furniture with a white sheet.

THE ARRANGEMENT

Images in botanical art traditionally show a plant illuminated from the upper-left side. This is appropriate for artists who are right-handed. The window should be located to the upper-left of the plant with the plant sitting on a table beside it. The artist should sit to the front, but slightly to the right of the plant, facing the easel or drawing board (if the artist is seated directly to the right of the plant only the shadow side of the plant is visible). When a freestanding easel is used, the paint, palette and water should be located on a separate table situated to the right of the artist. If a drawing board table is used, the materials should be located on the right side of the table surface. This arrangement allows for a clear observation of both the plant and the painting, and a system of looking from plant to picture to palette flows along unimpeded. Moreover, it prevents the painter's hand from shading the picture as it is painted. A mirror image of this arrangement is necessary for left-handed artists, to result in a picture of a plant that is illuminated from the upper-right.

DAYLIGHT

Light from a north-facing window is the most agreeable because it is cool, constant and does not cast any hard shadows upon the plant. Light from a window that faces any other direction will cast a hard shadow at some point during the day. You can screen a window with tracing or tissue paper to overcome this problem. For the sake of continuity of colour and tone, it is preferable not to change from daylight to lamplight when painting. It is better to use one or the other, or a constant combination of both.

LIGHT FITTINGS

A lamp provides light when daylight is not available, or if the quality of the daylight is poor. An adjustable angle-poise lamp that attaches securely to the table-top will supply a controlled light source to direct towards the plant. A strip light attached vertically to the wall (preferably in a corner) can provide a broader illumination, which will imitate window light. When working at night, a second angle-poise lamp may be needed, to illuminate the drawing board.

LIGHT BULBS

A blue-coloured Daylight Bulb emulates daylight, and is obtainable from art shops. The more sophisticated Phillips TLD95 is a full spectrum tube light, containing the total amount of light rays that are necessary to simulate daylight. It complies with the requirements made by the European Standard ISO 3664. These are available from specialist lighting companies who manufacture art conservation equipment. The warm tint of a standard domestic light bulb has an adverse effect on the natural colour of a plant; it is therefore advisable to avoid using this type. To eliminate any hard shadows cast by lamplight, place some tracing or tissue paper over the shade, ensuring that the paper does not touch the bulb. See Suppliers Directory for information on lighting products.

6 The Properties of Watercolour

FORMULATION AND PIGMENT TYPE

Watercolour paint is mainly composed of finely ground pigment and a binder. The binder is usually a type of gum arabic, known as gum kordofan. Glycerine, glucose, water and stabilisers are added to this combination, in proportions that are determined by the type of pigment. The paint is diluted with water before use, and is dry when the water has evaporated. This fast drying capacity allows the rapid application of successive layers of paint, and readily accommodates the transient nature of flowering plants. All watercolour paint is transparent when mixed with water, but the character of the pigment varies from colour to colour. Pigments are distinguished as Transparent, Semi-Opaque, or Opaque. The opaque colours, such as cadmium red are more substantial, more robust and possess the greatest covering power. The more delicate Transparent colours, such as raw umber, cover less well. It is regular practice to combine all three types of pigment when mixing colours or overlaying washes. Some colours, such as French ultramarine, show a marked tendency to granulate when combined with water, producing a characteristic pitted effect. Modern organic pigments made from petroleum derivatives, such as permanent rose, have a strong staining power. These produce intense colour that sinks well into the paper surface, staining it in the process. All paints categorised as Artist's Colours are classified as either Extremely Permanent; Permanent; Moderately Durable; or Fugitive. The Fugitive pigments are unstable and should be avoided. The ASTM abbreviation (present on the label) represents the American Society for Testing & Materials. This sets standards for the performance of materials, which includes the lightfastness of paint. ASTM I and II are rated as permanent, although not all artist's colours from the major manufacturers have been tested.

TRANSPARENCY AND BRILLIANCE

Transparency is the key characteristic of watercolour paint. When combined with water it yields translucent glazes that are applied as thin veils of colour. These colours shine through one another when overlaid. The reflected light of the white paper illuminates the layers of paint, transforming washes of pure colour into paler tints. This is particularly obvious with the red and magenta colours, which are laid thinly to produce pinks. In addition, watercolour allows the creation of intense, brilliant colours and dark tones, enabling the artist to render the richness of plant colour alongside the filmy tissue of petals and young leaves.

ACTING POWER AND FINE CONSISTENCY

Watercolours merge naturally and have a flowing quality, known as 'acting power'. This allows the creation of a smooth flat wash, with no evidence of brush marks. The refined consistency of the paint facilitates dry brush work, which brings detail to the work. The flower painter combines these two techniques to describe a plant's overall form and individual characteristics.

THE PURIST METHOD

The purist method of watercolour painting prescribed in this handbook employs the white of the paper to produce pale colours and highlights. Many artists favour the alternative method, which includes white watercolour or white gouache, which is mixed with the watercolour to produce pale tints and increase the opacity of the paint. The purist method preserves the quality of transparency that is inherent in the watercolour, and is arguably the most appropriate method because it empathises with the soft translucent textures of flowering plants.

7 Watercolour Wash Techniques

DAMPING THE PAPER

The specific quality of the wash is influenced by the size of brush, the opacity of the paint, the dilution of the wash, and whether it is painted onto wet, damp or dry paper.

The natural merging quality of watercolour paint is accentuated by a wet paper surface. This 'wet on wet' method causes the paint to bleed, as in Figure a. When the paper condition is damp or dry, rather than wet, the watercolour can be managed with the brush to produce a flat, smooth and even wash. The very first layers of wash always operate more successfully when the paper is damp. This softens the size on the paper surface, encouraging it to absorb the paint more readily.

Figure a

To damp the paper in preparation for a wash, paint clean clear water onto the area to be painted, using the appropriate size brush, and sweeping evenly. When the surface ceases to be very wet and shiny, it indicates that the water has been absorbed into the paper, leaving the surface damp. This is the right time to apply the wash. It is essential to allow each layer of paint to dry before another is laid over it. If a wash is painted onto one that is not dry, the brush effectively lifts the paint up from the first layer. Damping

Left 4 *Iris pallida*

the paper between washes is not essential, but is preferable on large areas of transparent petal, such as those of *Iris pallida* (Fig 4).

MIXING THE WASH

Always maintain two containers of water - one is for cleaning the brush and the other is for use in mixing paint. Always ensure that the brush is clean before using it to mix the wash. Place the paint onto the palette and add the water by degrees, mixing thoroughly. Avoid using a small brush to mix a large amount of wash. Generally, a wash is of the correct dilution if the white surface of the palette is still visible beneath a brush stroke of wash. The dilution of the wash can vary from a very thin to a richer consistency, depending on what is required for the painting. Always mix too much wash upon the palette, rather than too little. This saves any interruption for the mixing of more paint during the laying down of a wash.

LOADING THE BRUSH WITH WASH

A Nº 5 brush is appropriate for general work on areas no larger than 16cm² (2¼ sq in) approximately. For areas smaller than 1cm², a Nº 3 brush is suitable. A Nº 6 brush is necessary for areas of flat wash larger than 16cm².

The brush needs to absorb enough wash to cause it to expand without dripping. An overloaded brush cannot be shaped to a point, and an under-loaded brush will show very little sign of swelling. Dab a full brush on a piece of kitchen paper to absorb any excess wash, and always re-load the brush before it runs completely dry. If a painted section shows a dark contour around the edge, this denotes that the brush was over-loaded, as in Figure b. In effect, the paper is unable to absorb all the wash, and the tension in the excess water draws the pigment toward the edges of the painted area, where it dries as a dark line.

Figure b

Figure c, showing a wash displaying too many brush marks, indicating that the brush is too dry.

USING THE BRUSH

The best place to hold the brush, for ease of control, is where the metal ferrule meets the wooden handle. This applies for washes as well as dry brushwork (see Chapter 8). Hold the brush with the thumb and forefinger, resting it onto the third finger. It should make an angle of about 45° with the paper surface. Move the brush consistently, with a gentle flowing motion. Work decisively and avoid being too tentative, but do not press too hard with the brush. Work continuously until the specific area being covered is finished. Never stop and work backwards over a wash in an attempt to even out any inconsistencies. This serves to disturb the paper surface even further. A perfect wash is attainable, but it is not completely necessary. With the layering of washes, the painted surface evens out and any minor inconsistencies tend to disappear.

APPLICATION OF TECHNIQUES

The number of washes will vary from one to five, according to need. Opaque paint will usually require fewer layers than semi-opaque to achieve the same depth of colour. Initially, paint sinks into the paper; layers then begin to accumulate on top of the paper surface. If too many layers are applied to the paper, the surface becomes rough and muddy and the paint loses its brilliance.

The order of the application of washes and dry brushwork will vary according to the plant that is being painted. Recognition of the structure, colour and surface texture of the plant is always the best guide to determining precisely what techniques to use and

when to apply them. On the majority of occasions, once the drawing is complete, the washes are laid down as a foundation and dry brushwork is applied over this. However, there are exceptions to this rule, and in some circumstances, the dry brush techniques are applied before the washes or between the washes. In the flowers of *Tulipa* cultivar and *Canna* 'Wyoming', in Part II, the dry brushwork is fused between the layers of wash. This corresponds to the way the veining network exists within the tissue of the petals and sepals.

Mistakes happen, but unlike oil or acrylic mediums, watercolour is not easily removed. It is always simpler to deal with a mistake if the paint is still wet, rather than dry. Flood mistakes with clean water from a clean brush, allow the water to soak into the paper, and press the wet area with some kitchen paper or white cotton cloth. This will lift some of the paint from the paper, but it is not a reliable method of removing all traces of colour, particularly if the paint has a strong staining ability. It is possible to lift some colour with a clean damp brush, but always avoid scrubbing during this process, which may disturb the smooth surface of the paper.

THE FOUR BASIC WASHES

The following four basic wash techniques form the basis of the floral watercolour. The basic brush movements, as shown in the demonstration of the flat wash, are the same for the additional three washes, which are all variations of this principal method. Use a combination of the following wash techniques to build the overall form of the plant.

THE FLAT WASH

For a square the size of the one to the right, use a N° 5 brush. For this first layer of wash, dampen the area inside the square.

Using both the tip and side of the brush, lay a wide brush stroke of wash, working along the top of the square and moving left to right, as in Figure a*.

Continue the wash, travelling horizontally beside the first line, in the opposite direction, and slightly overlapping it. Keep the end of the brush just inside the edge of the first line, to allow the second line to merge with the first, as in Figure b.

Proceed with the wash, creating a smooth, uniform surface of colour, until the square is complete, as in Figures c to f.

Practising this technique within a square is of benefit when learning to gain control of the brush. Naturally, areas of all shapes and sizes are encountered when painting a plant. Adapt the above method to a plant form by tracking the edge of the petal, leaf, stem etc., with the tip and edge of the brush, whilst moving across the shape from one side to another, from the top to the bottom, or from top left to bottom right.

* Left-handed artists may find it more comfortable to work from right to left.

Figure a

Figure b

Figure c

Figure d

Figure e

Figure f

29

THE OVERLAID WASH

The overlaying of flat washes increases the depth and intensity of the colour. When first layered, a red, for example, will be a pinkish colour, which requires successive layers to become an intense red colour. Each wash must be dry before the following one is applied. Colours made from more than one colour are usually mixed on the palette before they are painted onto the paper. Even so, it is sometimes useful to overlay different colours onto the paper. The first colour will shine through the second colour, and the two will meld to produce a third colour, as in Figure g. On most occasions, for the best effects, darker, richer colours should be laid over the paler lighter colours.

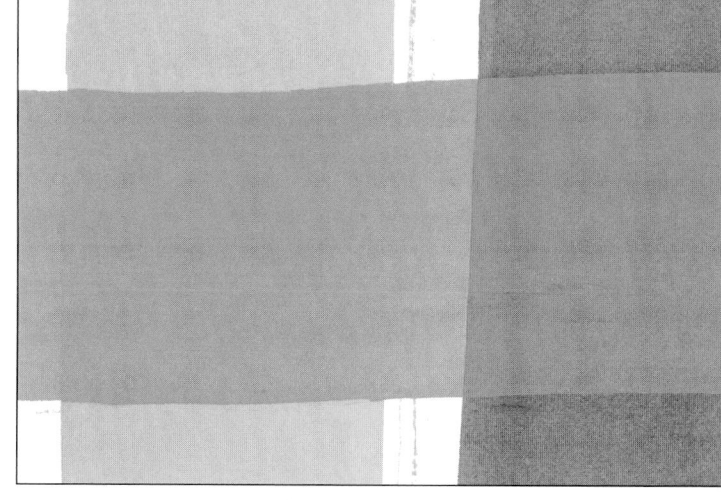

Figure g

THE GRADED WASH

Figure h

This technique fades a colour wash into a highlight, creating soft gradations of colour. Initially, apply a flat wash to dry or damp paper, and, at the point where the grading is required, clean the brush quickly, and load the brush with clean water only. Continue to paint, with the same brush strokes as before. The water will merge with the colour wash, which will appear to fade into the paper, as in Figure h. When dry, overlay the same technique, until the required depth of colour is achieved, as in Figure i. Here, the brush strokes are worked vertically from left to right.

Figure i

THE BLENDED WASH

Figure j

This technique blends together combinations of harmonious or discordant colour, as in Figure j. It uses the basic flat wash technique, but substitutes one colour for another colour at the appropriate place. When a different colour is required, clean the brush and load it quickly with the new colour. Blend this with the first colour using the same basic brush movements, to encourage the colours to merge.

Top 5a
Lilium lancifolium 'Flore Pleno'

Below left 5b
Florists' *Chrysanthemum* (reflexed form)

Below right 5c
Florists' *Chrysanthemum* (reflexed form)

Both 5b and 5c show combinations of graded and blended washes.

8 Dry Brush Techniques

THE USES FOR DRY BRUSH

Traditional methods of dry brush work compliment the watercolour washes by providing the means to model a surface, describe fine detail and texture, and delineate venation. The dry brush is essentially a damp brush, which is moderately loaded with paint. This facilitates an exacting process of painting minutiae at a slower pace than wash work. The techniques use the tip of the brush, but not the side of the brush. An excessive amount of dry brush work across the entire image tends to create an unnatural appearance, but the appropriate use of the techniques brings a picture to life. Dry brush work is generally painted upon a foundation of wash work, but some may be applied in thin dilute paint between washes. When the paper surface holds dense dry brush work, it is not possible to lay further washes over it without the inevitable disruption of detail.

MIXING PAINT AND LOADING THE BRUSH

Initially, mix the paint on the palette to the required thickness - as dilute wash or more condensed paint - depending on the technique. As dry brush is less rapid than wash work, only small areas can be painted at any one time, therefore, less paint is needed on the palette. Mixing may continue during painting without adversely affecting the progress of the work. Hold the dry brush in the same way as for a wash. Dip the brush into the paint mixture, and load it so that it shows signs of expanding, but to a lesser degree than for a wash. Reduce any excess by brushing the tip onto a spare piece of watercolour paper, kitchen paper, or cotton paint rag. A brush that is too dry will run out of paint after a few short strokes, and the procedure will become unnecessarily slow. Always reshape the tip of the brush before use. The precise shape differs with each of the following dry brush methods:

MODELLING DRY BRUSH

This method is essentially for the building of dense shading (Figures 5b and 5c on page 31) and the modelling of surface areas, such as Figure a, a detail of the bud of *Camellia japonica* 'Adolphe Audusson' in Part II. This technique generally constitutes the final layers of a painting. A №5 (Figure b), or №3 brush, are the most appropriate. A №1 has insufficient hairs. A №6 may be useful for modelling large leaves, such as in Figure 7 (on page 38).

Load the brush, shape the tip into a chisel shape (Figure b), and apply the paint in small strokes. For modelling petals and leaves, and creating shading between leaf veining, lay the brush strokes facing in one direction, either horizontally or vertically. In Figure 7, the shading on the *Monstera deliciosa* leaf was applied between the sections of veining, in a vertical direction. Apply this technique to dry or damp paper, and blend the strokes softly together, so that no hard edges are apparent. To avoid a hard edge on the dry brush mass, grade it with the brush using clean water. Layer the brush strokes from light to dark to achieve depth of shade. To build a velutinous surface (Figure a), create a mesh of texture with brush strokes that face in various directions.

Figure a

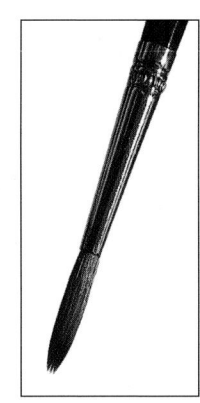

Figure b

POINTED DRY BRUSH

This method is useful for creating fine detail and small areas of surface texture. Figure c shows the orange stamens of *Lilium longiflorum* 'Mount Everest' (in Part II) that were built-up with small brush strokes. In Figure 5a, the spots on the *Lilium lancifolium* were created from building up dots of pointed dry brush. This technique, when required, forms the finishing layers of the painting. The most suitable brush is a Nº 3 (Figure d), or Nº1 (Figure h). Shape the brush tip to a sharp point, and apply miniature strokes or dots of paint onto a dry surface. Build the detail in layers, using the thickest paint at the end of the process.

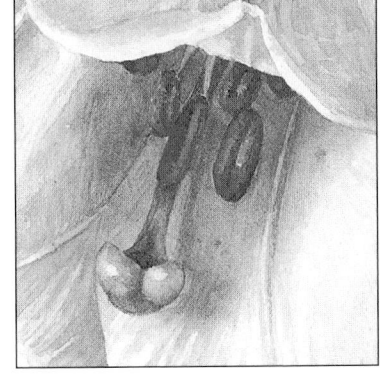

Figure c

Figure d

SWEEPING DRY BRUSH

This method produces a textural impression of parallel veining, ridging or long lines of pigmentation on a plant surface, such as Figure e, a detail of the *Tulipa* cultivar in Part II. When drawing with a Nº1 brush to delineate every single vein or mark is impractical, and results in a laboured appearance, this technique provides an alternative. To separate the hair tips and produce a fan-like shape (Figure f), load the brush, then apply pressure to the heel of the brush (where the hairs join the metal ferrule) on the surface of the palette. Then, sweep the hairs gently across the paper in one stroke. Connect the sweeping strokes by laying them alongside one another, taking care to space each sweep evenly. Apply with dilute paint, onto damp or dry paper. Place between washes, over washes, or onto clean paper.

Figure e

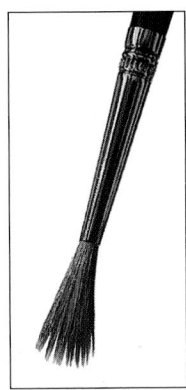

Figure f

DRAWING DRY BRUSH

This method is used principally for delineation, such in Figure g - a detail of veining in the *Anemone coronaria* 'The Admiral', in Part II. The most appropriate brush is a Nº 1, but a Nº3 or a Nº5 brush is useful for painting larger veins and features. A single layer of line work made from slightly richer paint is preferable, as over painting in thin washes may diminish the accuracy of the drawing. Shape the brush to a fine point (Figure h), and draw the lines onto dry or damp paper. Apply as a final layer, or integrate line between washes. Drawing on damp paper creates a softer line, useful for the veining of some petals, such as those of *Canna* 'Wyoming' in Part II.

Figure g

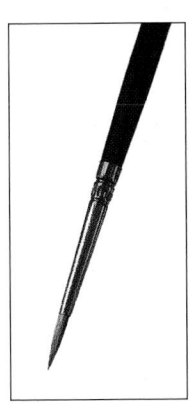

Figure h

9 The Colour Palette

Painters generally use the three basic primary colours, which are red, yellow and blue, to mix all other colours. This approach, along with the many other methods of colour mixing that employ a limited palette, is of benefit to many artists. However, flower painters require more than three primaries to achieve the full spectrum of colours found in the plant kingdom. We can extend our options for colour mixing by employing two reds, two yellows, and two blues. This allows us to utilise our natural ability to distinguish warm colours from cool colours, and each pair of the following primary colours is specifically chosen to demonstrate a warm/cool polarity. These are effective for painting the subtle colour contrasts observable in flowers, stems and leaves.

Cadmium Red (warm)	&	**Permanent Alizarin Crimson** (cool)	= **Red Primaries**
Cadmium Yellow (warm)	&	**Cadmium Lemon** (cool)	= **Yellow Primaries**
Cerulean Blue (warm)	&	**French Ultramarine** (cool)	= **Blue Primaries**

Warm primaries reflect more light from the red end of the spectrum, and cool primaries reflect more light from the blue end of the spectrum, hence the association of colour with temperature. All colour assessment is relative. Cadmium red is the warmest colour in the collection. Cadmium yellow is cooler than cadmium red and permanent alizarin crimson, but warmer than cadmium lemon and both blues. French ultramarine is the coolest colour in the collection. Cerulean blue is warm in relation to French ultramarine, but cooler than both reds and both yellows.

Cadmium Red
Permanent / ASTM I Opaque
Staining pigment. Excellent covering power.
A very warm, intense bright red. Granulating.
Particularly good for mixing rich oranges.

Permanent Alizarin Crimson
Permanent Transparent
Staining pigment. Good covering power.
A cool bluish-red.
Invaluable for pinks in thin washes.

Cadmium Yellow
Permanent / ASTM I Opaque
Staining pigment. Excellent covering power.
A very warm, clear orange-yellow.
Good for mixing rich greens.

Cadmium Lemon
Permanent / ASTM I Opaque
Staining pigment. Excellent covering power.
A cool, pale greenish-yellow.
Good for mixing light greens and oranges.

Cerulean Blue
Extremely Permanent / ASTM I Semi-Opaque
Non-staining pigment. Weak covering power.
A warm, light greenish-blue. Granulating.
Indispensable for mixing bright clear greens.

French Ultramarine
Permanent / ASTM I Transparent
Non-staining pigment. Good covering power.
A cool, rich violet-blue. Granulating.
Essential for a variety of rich, dark greens.

ADDITIONAL BRIGHT COLOURS FOR FLOWER PAINTING

The secondary colours are produced from a mixture of primary colours. These are orange (red+yellow), green (yellow+blue), and violet (blue+red). Our warm/cool range of primary colours offers the potential for a variety of mixtures of corresponding warm/cool secondary colours, but the purple and violet mixtures are not as bright as those found in nature. In addition, mixing does not produce the intense pink and magenta colours that are found in some flora. Therefore, the following additional colours are recommended to complete the range:

Permanent Rose
Permanent /ASTM I Transparent
Staining pigment. Good covering power.
A cool, intense pink.
Excellent for pale pink glazes.

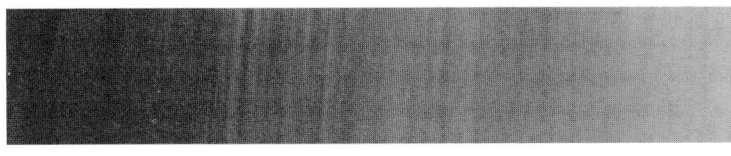

Quinacridone Magenta
Permanent   Transparent
Staining pigment. Good covering power.
A cool, intense violet-pink.
Suitable for the coolest pinks.

Permanent Magenta
Permanent/ASTM I Transparent
Staining pigment. Good covering power.
A cool, dull, magenta.
Mix with reds for rich plum colours.

Winsor Violet (Dioxazine)
Permanent Transparent Staining pigment.
Good covering power.
A mid-tone, intense violet.
Excellent for pale and dark violets.

EARTH COLOURS FOR FLOWER PAINTING

The yellow, brown and red colours made from earth pigments are naturally dull but distinctive in character. These have the ability to subdue bright colours, particularly greens and oranges.

Yellow Ochre
Extremely Permanent/ASTM I Opaque
Non-staining pigment. Transparent in glazes.
A warm, dull yellow.
Useful for calming bright yellows.

Raw Umber
Extremely Permanent/ASTM I Transparent
Non-staining pigment. Weak covering power.
A cool, greenish brown. Granulating.
Good for mixing brownish greens.

Burnt Sienna
Extremely Permanent ASTM/I Transparent
Non-staining pigment. Weak covering power.
A warm, bright reddish brown.
Excellent for woody stems and buds.

6 *Magnolia grandiflora*

10 Mixing Greens

The world of flowering plants flourishes with an infinite variety of greens, from the bright and acid, and the cool and glaucous, to the pale and light, and the rich and dark. Close inspection of any individual plant can reveal a complex verdancy that cannot be represented by a ready mixed green from a tube or pan. Certain colours such as Sap Green, Viridian and Hooker's Green have their place, but they often impart a sense of unnatural brilliance that will need neutralising before it can correlate with a living plant. The green colours mixed from the six primary colours are not only harmonious, but also natural in appearance.

The following four basic mixtures of green are produced from the primary colours. Each green range is a mixture of two colours only, and is prone toward cooler bluish green on the left side, and warmer yellowish green on the right side. The central area shows the true green colour. The fifth basic green uses yellow ochre, which has little strength when combined with most blues, but produces an excellent glaucous green when mixed with cerulean blue. Extend the subtlety of these mixtures by combining two blues and one yellow, or two yellows and one blue.

Cadmium Lemon + French Ultramarine
Mid-green mix. A ubiquitous green that combines well with Neutral Tint.
See the foliage in Figure 7.

Cadmium Lemon + Cerulean Blue
Intense green mix. A delicate colour that works well in thin glazes. See the stem of *Tulipa* Florist's hybrid in Part II.

Cadmium Yellow + French Ultramarine
Sombre green mix.
Good depth of colour for rich deep greens.
See the foliage in Figure 6.

Cadmium Yellow + Cerulean Blue
Warm green mix.
Strong in character, but not overtly bright.
See buds of *Lilium longiflorum* in Part II.

Yellow Ochre + Cerulean Blue
Glaucous green mix.
Limited variation but with a definite use.
See the leaves in Figure 3.

11 The Neutral Tint Mixture

Each colour possesses a tonal value, and there are a number of ways to darken a bright hue. Colours are reduced when mixed with their so-called complementary or opposite colours, but this usually leads to a brown or grey mixture that has little substantial depth. Combining a colour with a ready mixed black, such as Lamp Black or Ivory Black will be more effective in shading it, but this will make the colour muddy. A mixture composed of three primary colours produces the most viable black that effectively neutralises or darkens colours without corrupting them. Figure 7 *Monstera deliciosa* shows a foliage colour that was darkened with Neutral Tint. The combination of French ultramarine, permanent alizarin crimson and cadmium yellow produces a dark blackish tone, traditionally known as the Neutral Tint mixture. This is useful for producing several colours that are required by the flower painter, as well as for monochrome painting. Neutral tint affects a colour by subtle degrees, and requires addition in small doses, as too much or not enough may entirely alter the balance of the colour. It is normal for this mixture to separate and granulate in thin washes.

THE METHOD FOR MIXING NEUTRAL TINT
Initially, place French ultramarine onto the palette. This colour is the main compound of the mixture. To this add permanent alizarin crimson, to create a bluish violet colour (a). The approximate amount is four parts French ultramarine to one part permanent alizarin crimson. The amount of paint required varies according to the brand, so the precise colour is discernible by eye. Thereafter, add the cadmium yellow sparingly, until a steady black appears (b). Mix the combination thoroughly to create the dark velvety black (c).

The careful amalgamation of the three colours cancels out the colour value of each one, absorbs all the light, and produces a dense black. The use of paint from a pan or block results in a thinner, more dilute consistency. A substantial amount can be mixed from tube paint in a small ceramic dish. If covered in plastic film, this will keep for several weeks without drying out. An old paintbrush is useful for mixing the paint; however, a small flexible metal palette knife is more appropriate for larger amounts of tube paint.

Figure a

Figure b

Figure c

Left 7 *Monstera deliciosa*

8a *Paeonia lactiflora* 'Sarah Bernhardt'

8b *Rosa* 'Mme. Ernst Calvat'

8c Florists' *Chrysanthemum* (reflexed form)

8d *Dianthus* cultivar

12 Colour Assessment

EVALUATION

You should evaluate the colour that exists within a living plant before mixing the equivalent on the palette. An analytical approach to the diagnosis of individual colours simplifies this complex process. Every colour in the visible spectrum has three main attributes. These are Hue, Saturation, and Tonal Value. Colour assessment becomes easier, faster and more accurate when the observation is broken down into these three principles.

HUE

This describes the basic essential colour visible in a plant or in paint pigment. It appears to the eye as any kind of red, orange, yellow, green, blue, violet, or magenta.

SATURATION

This term indicates the strength of any hue visible in a plant or a paint pigment. A rich colour has a high saturation, but this is diminished when the colour is paler, greyer or darker. Mixing a small amount of neutral tint with a hue effectively reduces its saturation, making it less bright. The duller pinks found in the petals of the flowers in Fig 8 a,b,c and d were created by adding neutral tint to cadmium red, permanent magenta and permanent rose. A brilliant red flower, such as a poppy, contains highly saturated reds. A pale pink rose may contain the same hue of red, but it will have a lower saturation because it is diluted with white. In actuality, as a hue becomes lighter or darker the colour saturation always decreases.

TONAL VALUE

This denotes the lightness or darkness of any particular hue visible in a plant or a paint pigment. Tonal Value distinguishes a lighter from a darker colour. A dark green and a brilliant green may be of the same hue, but the brilliant green is tonally lighter. A plant will reflect the surrounding light, and this will inevitably affect the colour. When a plant with a large complex leaf arrangement is illuminated from one light source, the leaves furthest away from the light or those in deep shadow will appear to possess a colour with less light value. The colour of the leaves located in the bright light, and in particular the highlighted areas, will appear to have a lighter tonal value.

COLOUR MIXING

Hue and saturation indicate the qualities of a colour and light value refers to the amount of colour that is present. When mixing colours to correspond with those observed within a plant, firstly evaluate the hue and then its level of saturation. Thereafter, assess the light value of each individual colour, by observing it in flat light away from bright sun or deep shade.

TINTS

A pale or pastel colour is known as a tint. This type of colour has a low saturation and a high light value. In mediums such as oil, acrylic and gouache, we add white paint to a rich hue to produce a tint. In watercolour, we allow the whiteness of the paper to act as a lightener and create the tint. For this we simply dilute the paint, and lay down a thin wash of colour. To produce a tint in this way we must first decide what hue we require. For example, a red or deep pink hue from a tube or pan will create a pastel pink when diluted with water and painted as one layer of wash. In Figure 8 a, b, c and d, the palest tints were made with thin dilutions of cadmium red, permanent magenta and permanent rose. Where the richer hues of more saturated pink were needed, more layers of colour were overlaid, using washes with a higher concentration of paint.

Shades

A shade is a darker tone of any pure hue. This type of colour has a low saturation and a low light value. The simplest way for us to create a shade is to add neutral tint to a pure hue, which darkens the tone of the colour. Shades for oil, acrylic and gouache are produced in the same way. The dark green of the leaf in Fig 7(page 38) began with a basic green hue consisting of French ultramarine and cadmium lemon. Thereafter, neutral tint was added to achieve the dark shade.

The tint and shade scale

A brilliant cadmium red hue has the highest saturation possible in terms of colour value. Tonally it is darker than cadmium lemon, which has a relatively lower saturation in comparison, but a higher level of light. The tint and shade scale below is composed of the six primaries from Chapter 9, with the three cool hues on the left and the three warm hues on the right. The pure hue is located along the centre of each scale.

The tint scale works from the centre of the scale upwards, where each hue was blended towards white with a graded wash. Each colour becomes lighter in tonal value as it becomes more dilute. Both yellow hues move towards the light the quickest because of their high light value. French ultramarine and permanent alizarin crimson take longer to become lighter because they are darker in tone.

The shaded scale works from the pure hue downwards, where each colour is darkened with the gradual addition of neutral tint. The cadmium red takes the longest to shade because of its high saturation and good covering power. The French ultramarine takes less time than the cadmium lemon to shade deeply, because of its natural dark tone as a pigment.

A scale of this kind can be extended to include all kinds of secondary colours, other bright colours, and earth colours. This useful exercise combines tonal colour mixing with the graded and blended wash techniques. To produce the tint scale, paint the pure hue onto watercolour paper, and grade the wash with water. Use a N° 5 or N° 6 brush, grading the paint in one direction, away from the hue. To create the shaded portion of the scale, mix the hue with neutral tint on the palette. Thereafter, place some more pure hue beside the first, in the central area of the scale, and, working in the opposite direction, blend this with the mixture from the palette, to achieve a gradual darkening of the colour.

Tint Scale

Pure Hue

Shade Scale

Right   9 Tint and shade scales of *Rosa* 'Mme. Ernst Calvat'.

13 Drawing

OBSERVATION

It is not necessary to be a botanist to be able to draw and paint flowers. Nevertheless, a little botanical knowledge supplies information about the characteristics that typify a plant, or distinguish it from other plants. Some basic understanding of the structure and life cycle of the angiosperms will always be of benefit to the flower painter, in the same way that the study of human anatomy is useful to the artist who paints the human figure.

To the best of your ability, draw what you can honestly see is present, and refrain from including any elements that are assumed, imagined or invented. This method of observational drawing relies upon an ongoing assessment of how one part of a plant exists in relation to another part. Moreover, through this kind of investigative process, we acquire knowledge about a plant and develop familiarity with it.

The following methods provide a systematic approach to drawing that helps to minimise the struggle for accuracy. An entire drawing can be built around a single mistake, therefore it is worth taking the time to remedy a fault as soon as you discover it. Regular checking is necessary, and if it is practical, erase the incorrect lines and draw them again before continuing with the rest of the work. When a majority of the drawing requires alteration, it may be more appropriate to discard the work and begin again on a fresh piece of paper.

THE PENCIL LINE DRAWING

In naturalistic flower painting, a pencil is used to make an outline drawing of a plant. This may be part of any preliminary work, or a precise drawing that precedes a piece of highly finished work, such as those in Part II. In all of this drawing work, the pencil line defines the edges and extremities of the whole plant form, and constructs the parts of it that overlap or coincide. It also marks the areas where a junction of parts occurs, such as where a leaf, bract, bud or flower, join a stem. In addition, line provides other structural detail, such as the venation of leaves and petals. It may also be of use to indicate where one colour ends and another begins. In total, the pencil drawing becomes a linear map of the visible characteristics of a plant.

In a Thumbnail Sketch, the pencil is used to outline the essential elements of the plant on a small scale. In a Tonal Sketch, a Colour Study, and a precision drawing that is the basis of a highly finished painting, the pencil line creates a framework for the watercolour. This is rather like a skeleton over which the flesh of the paint is built. In this way, the drawing is not an end in itself, but part of a whole process. Sketches, and studies, are working drawings and it is only necessary to erase construction lines if their presence is a distraction. Preliminary work should be done swiftly, and with practice, it will become possible to draw a general impression of a plant with a few lines. Detail is not as vital to this work as it is to the drawing made for a finished painting, which contains more information. Never over embroider with pencil work, as this may easily result in a painting with a laboured appearance.

PAPER SIZE

Always allow enough paper space around a sketch, study or finished drawing. For preliminary work, this offers room for the development of additional ideas, more sketching, annotation, and experimental colour mixtures. For a precise drawing that forms the basis of a painting, allow a border of at least 50mm (2in. approximately), beyond the edge of the work. This gives a margin for mounting and framing, and ensures that no marks occur on the drawing from any handling of the work.

USING THE PENCIL

When drawing, place a light piece of blotting paper beneath your drawing hand to protect the paper from any marks made by your hand. The piece of paper need only be approximately 130x 250mm (5x10in.). If the drawing board is on an upright easel, this should be taped to the edge of the drawing board to stop it from falling. As you move your hand during the drawing process, adjust the placement of the blotting paper. In addition, have beside you a small piece of paper (the same brand as you are drawing on) and use this to practice pencil strokes on and to loosen up your drawing hand before beginning work.

The hard H pencil is suitable for a drawing that precedes a finished painting, and the slightly softer HB pencil is appropriate for faster sketching and study work. Both of these grades can take a fine point, and neither will smudge easily. Sharpen the pencil to a fine point, preferably with a craft knife, which is more efficient than a pencil sharpener. Hold the pencil 30-50mm (1-2in.) approximately, from the beginning of the lead. This is the most suitable position from which to control the pencil. Hold the pencil firmly, but do not grip it. Allow the pencil movements to originate from your upper arm and shoulder, as opposed to your fingers or wrist, which may lead to tension and strain. Rest your hand lightly onto the side of your little finger and glide your hand across the paper when drawing. Remember to breath regularly, because the quickening or holding of any breath results in a tentative and shaky drawing.

Draw with the point of the pencil rather than the side, and sharpen it as soon as it shows signs of becoming blunt. Press too hard with the pencil and the line will make an unpleasant indentation in the paper surface. Press too softly, and the drawing will be difficult to comprehend. Aim to draw in clear and sharp lines that are all of a similar thickness and density. All the lines that depict form should flow into one another and produce an agreeable whole. The seamless joining of short lines is often necessary to create the appearance of one uninterrupted line, such as those needed for a length of fleshy stem.

THE ERASER

Use a kneaded putty eraser, shaped into to a point, to remove any mistakes or lines that you do not want to keep. This type of malleable eraser is more effective than the hard plastic type that leaves behind debris. The putty eraser absorbs the pencil graphite, and the moulded point eventually becomes blackened with use. This blackened part must be removed to reveal the clean material, so that a new point may be moulded. Most drawing will show through delicate watercolour paint, therefore, a kneaded eraser is used to lighten a drawing without completely removing it. Gently pat the completed drawing with the eraser, to achieve this effect.

BASIC MEASUREMENTS WITH A RULER

All drawings in this book (apart from thumbnail sketches) are relatively life-size, to represent a plant in its natural state, and allow the development of all necessary detail. For a life-size drawing, utilise a transparent plastic ruler to establish the whole height and width of the area of the plant to be included in the drawing. This ruler needs to be long enough for these measurements. Hold the ruler close to the plant and in front of it, and then measure the total width and total height of the area. Place these measurements onto the paper as four boundary pencil lines. Join these to produce a large square or rectangle, as in Figures 10 and 11. This establishes the top, bottom, far left and far right of the drawing. Draw these lines with a ruler or free hand if a straight line is achievable.

After defining these boundary points, the measurements of the main parts of the plant (including blooms, stems, clusters of leaves, large buds, etc.) should be established. Ascertain these measurements by measuring inwards from the four boundary lines with a smaller ruler, held vertically or horizontally. Through this measuring, a series of pencil reference marks, or notches, are built onto the drawing to establish the basic height and width of these parts of the plant.

Extend these marks (by means of a ruler or steady freehand drawing) to form longer lines. These lines subsequently cross over one another at right angles producing boxes of various shapes and sizes, which represent the heights and widths of each part. Thereafter, construct each of the main parts within a box. Continue until the entire composition is complete, including the placing of other smaller details, such as the small buds, pistil, and stamens. Figure 10 shows a flowering stem of *Paeonia lactiflora* 'Sir Edward Elgar', in which the main flowers and large bud are drawn within boxes.

Always establish the general measurements before adding any details, and always work from the whole to the part. Flowers that die faster than leaves may have to be painted first, but it is necessary to determine the precise location of all parts of the plant before doing so. When measuring, take care not to slope the ruler toward or away from the plant, but to always hold it perpendicular and on the same imaginary level surface. This ensures that all the measurements accord with one another.

PROPORTION

When a plant is dissected and each part is measured, it can be drawn precisely life-size. Efforts to depict a growing plant life-size can only be relative or approximate, because plants occupy space and appear to alter in size as they recede from the eye. Measuring all the main parts of a plant ensures that each part is correct in relation to another part, and that all are proportionally accurate. The need for all parts of a plant to relate correctly may again be compared to a drawing of a human figure, which would obviously be inaccurate if it showed a foot to be the same length as the leg. It may require someone as knowledgeable as a botanist to recognise any faults present in a flower drawing. Therefore, the artist should strive to maintain truth to nature and commitment to observation, in order to make their work as accurate as possible.

It is usual to select one small but dominant part of a drawing, such as a prominent bloom, bud or a length of stem, and use this as a so-called 'constant'.

The constant is a reference to which all other parts can relate proportionally. In Figure 10, the drawing made for the Colour Study in Figure 17 (page 65), the width of the main bud was used as the constant. The width of the constant fits three times into the width of the main open bloom that is above the bud. The constant was also used to check the accuracy of other parts of the drawing.

In traditional observational drawing, a pencil is held out at arm's length to check proportions. When a pencil is employed in this way, it must always be held out from the eye at the same distance each time, to avoid discrepancies in any of the measurements. The thumb of the hand that is holding the pencil slides up and down it, and stops at the visible length or width of the part that is being used as the constant. The thumb is held in position, as the pencil is moved across to another part. The comparison is made between the constant held on the length of pencil, and the other part. The amount of times that the constant will fit into the other part is then determined by moving the pencil across the subject. The relationship of the two, in terms of proportion, then becomes established. This method is useful for checking a drawing during construction. With regular drawing practice, an eye for relative proportion develops, as does the ability to detect the cause of a fault.

In addition to drawing boxes, a window-viewfinder (see Chapter 15) is effective as a gauge for proportions, when divided into a grid. Draw the grid with a fine felt pen, onto clear acetate or a small piece of thin clear plastic or glass. Place this squarely over the window of the viewfinder and attach it, with strong sticky tape, to the border around the window. Choose the dimensions of a grid to suit the plant. It is useful to have a selection of viewfinders with different sized grids. Observe the plant through the grid, as in 'a' and 'b'. In 'a' the length and width of the *Camellia* leaf shows through the grid, which is emphasised in red. In 'b', the grid clarifies the position of the midrib.

Right 10 *Paeonia lactiflora* 'Sir Edward Elgar'

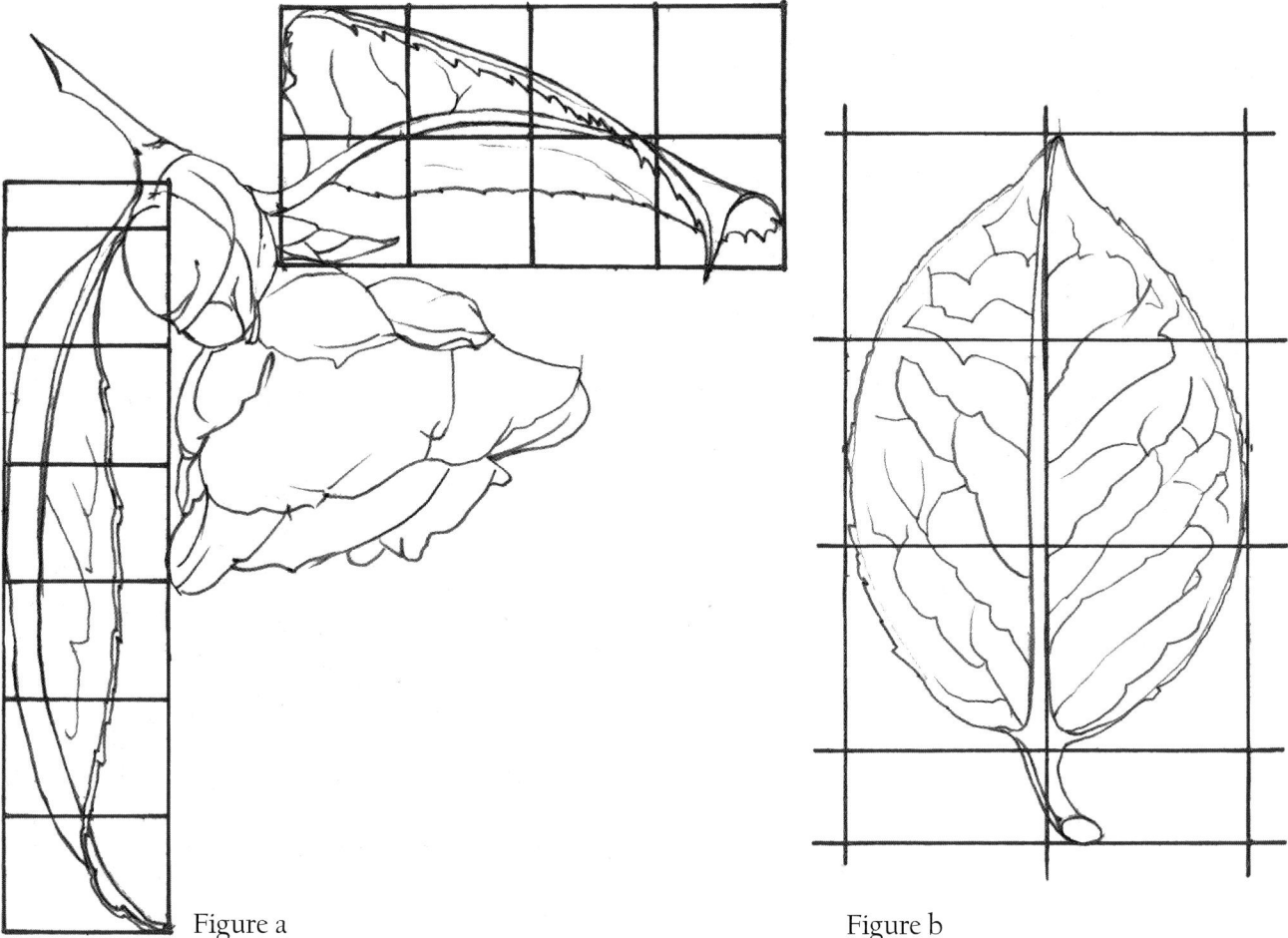

Figure a

Figure b

THE PLUMB LINE

The edges of the paper are a reference for a constant horizontal and vertical, but a plumb line is useful for establishing a true vertical in a plant. When the line is held up, the weight on the end of it holds the line in a true perpendicular. This instrument is invaluable for assessing and clarifying the positions of the various parts of a plant in relation to one another.

Hold up the plumb line in front of the plant, so that it is aligned with a part that has already been drawn, such as the edge of the flower. When we look up and down the plumb line, we see precisely what else is located along the same vertical line. The position of the vertical lines that represent where the plumb line is placed, are marked lightly onto to the paper with a ruler or by steady freehand. These marks act as additional reference points that will establish the correct location of the flowers, stems, and leaves etc. Regular

use of the plumb line eventually imprints an image of a perpendicular line upon the memory, and the plumb line will be required less often. It eventually becomes possible to cast an imaginary line with the mind and know instantly what is situated along it. Figure 11 (page 51) shows the beginnings of the drawing of *Canna* 'Wyoming', made for the final painting in Part II. The plumb line was used to secure the location of the petals and sepals in this complex group. To show where the plumb line was used, the lines have been extended and emphasised up and down the length of the drawing.

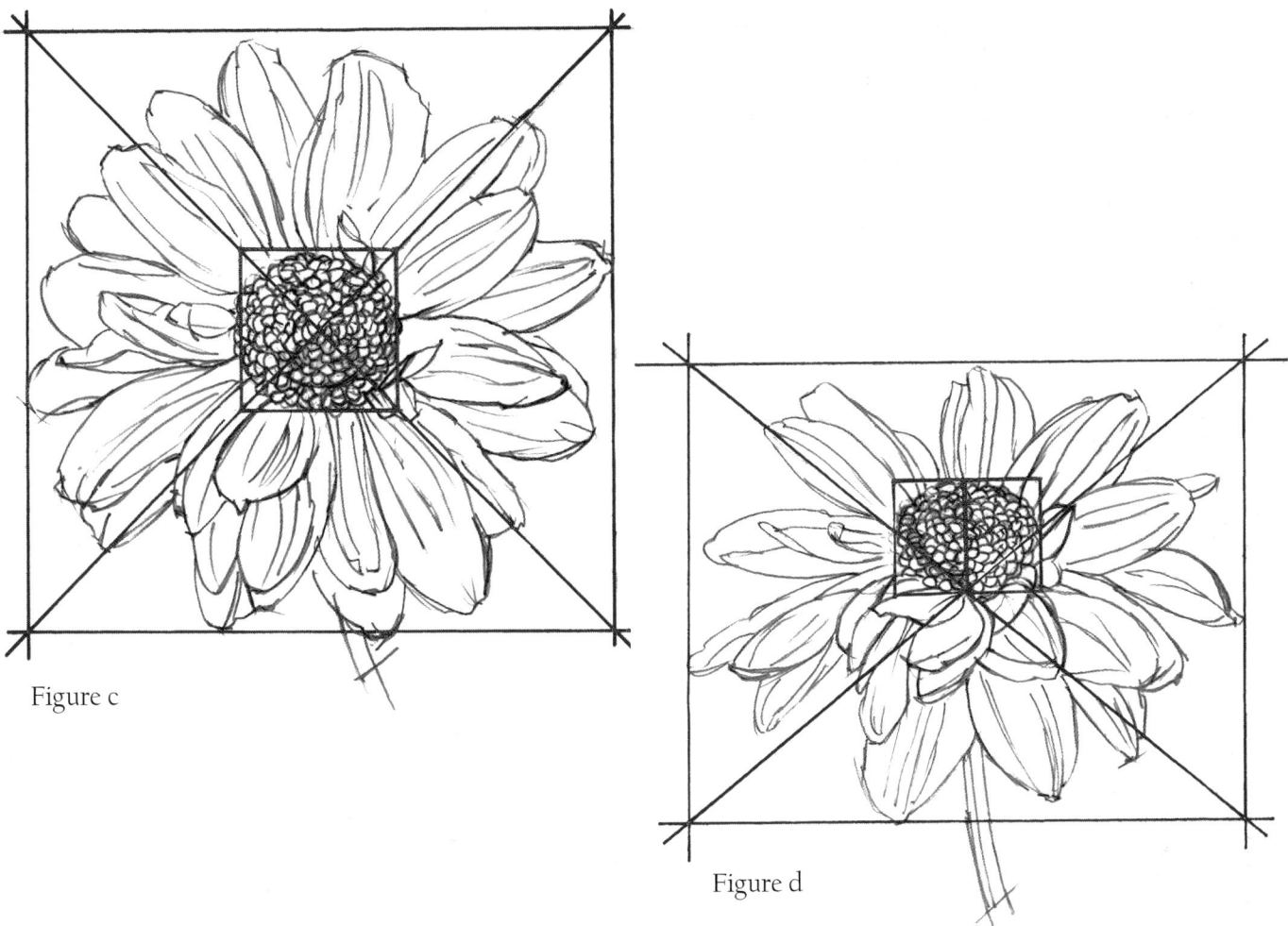

Figure c

Figure d

LINEAR PERSPECTIVE

Plants appear smaller at a distance than they do when near to us. Perspective is the term given to the creation of this illusion on a flat two-dimensional surface. When successful, it represents a plant in a three-dimensional reality, and brings the effective impression of space in a painting. When a circular flower, such as one from a spray of florists' chrysanthemums (c), is seen in full-face from the front, the appearance is of an entire circular shape. If we place the same flower flat on a table, or we look at it sideways, or from an above (d), we become aware of certain changes in the appearance of the form. The circular shape becomes a regular oval, known as an ellipse. In addition, the petals nearest to us appear to be larger than those farthest away, which is an occurrence known as foreshortening. Linear perspective is the term given to the combined changes in angles, shapes, and the direction of lines that occur as we observe them from our human position.

THE EYE LEVEL

When we alter our point of view, such as if we move from standing above a plant to sitting beside it, our perspective view also alters. The eye level is the term given to the height that the artist's eyes occupy in relation to the plant. The drawing always reflects the artist's personal eye level, and any spectator viewing a painting will see the plant as the artist chose to see it. A huge number of plants exist in nature below the height of the human eye. For a drawing or painting, these are usually raised up to our human level so that their characteristics may be more clearly seen.

PERSPECTIVE DRAWING

There will always be some amount of perspective seen in a plant, even if it is viewed precisely on the eye level. A drawing that ignores this fact will appear unnaturally flat. The construction of flowers, buds, leaves and stem shapes in perspective can be carried out in more than one way. One traditional method favours constructing flowers by relating them to a relevant geometric shape, such as a circle, cone, triangle, square, trapezium, diamond and star. The appropriate geometric shape is selected to suit the particular plant part, and this is constructed to a size corresponding to that of the flower. The flower is then drawn within this shape. As the majority of flowers display symmetry, this is a logical approach. Even so, this method can often be time consuming and more confusing to the artist, who may need to construct a geometric shape in perspective before the plant can be drawn within it.

This system therefore necessitates some technical drawing. This can be set aside for an equally effective method of drawing the plant by direct assessment of the height and width of the various parts of the plant (as we have seen), to which we add the drawing of the angles and curves that it displays. These angles and curves are necessary to the creation of the whole plant form, and, the method requires some further construction work, but none that is as complex as a geometric shape in perspective.

ANGLES AND THE CLOCK FACE METHOD

Many plant forms display angular shapes, which may be difficult to evaluate and translate into line. This might be the angle that a stamen makes as it rises from the centre of a flower, the angles at which petals overlap, the angles that the edges of leaves display as they twist through space in perspective, or the angle at which a stem grows upward from the ground, to name but a few. A protractor may be held up in front of the plant form to measure these angles, but a more expedient way is to assess it in terms of the hand of a clock. This is known as the 'Clock Face' Method. To determine the angle observed, relate it to the large hand of a clock. For example, a petal that grows out of a calyx at 90° to the right will be at number 3 on the clock face. In addition, the two

hands of a clock may be effectively used to establish the angles of an axil. All angles of the stems, and some angles of the leaves in Figure 10 (page 47), were assessed in this way.

DEFINING CURVES

All plant forms display curves, and all curves, particularly those in perspective, may be clearly assessed through their relationship to a straight line. A plumb line determines a vertical, and the upper and lower edges of the paper provide a constant horizontal reference. When either of these is related to a curve, the depth of the curve becomes clear. If necessary, a horizontal or vertical can be drawn onto the paper, and the curve constructed beside it. The curves of a circular, spherical or cup-shaped flower may be usefully compared to the square or rectangle in which they have been constructed. To secure an accurate circle or elliptical shape, divide a square or rectangular box into four equal triangles, by joining the four corners with two diagonal lines that cross at the centre of the flower, as in the drawings of the florists' chrysanthemum 'c' and 'd'. Two additional lines, one vertical and one horizontal, could be added, to cross over at the central point of the box. These must always begin and end mid-way along each side of the box, and cross over each other at the centre of the box. You can construct an accurately proportioned circle or ellipse within this structure by using these dividing lines as a guide, and building the curves from the four equal parts. The central point of the box will be where the stem or stalk connects to the flower head. To place the flower head correctly on its axis extend the central axis line. In 'd', a divided rectangle surrounds the central button-shape, helping to place each tiny, unopened disc floret in the correct position.

Right 11 *Canna* 'Wyoming'

Guidelines

The following guidelines offer a methodical working procedure for drawing particular parts of a plant. This indicates what requires observation, and how to define it in terms of drawing. It is most unlikely that any artist will mistake a stem for a flower, but the simple acknowledgement of the constituent parts of a plant and a recognition of the most suitable approach to drawing them, promotes clarity in the mind of the artist, and consequently in the drawing itself. Naturally, there exists a large range of typical shapes and arrangements of stems, leaves, flowers, buds, hairs, thorns and prickles, all of which may be constructed according to the previous recommendations for drawing. The roots are an indispensable part of the living plant, but are not included as the purpose of this book is to focus on parts of the plant that bloom, and are above ground level. A scientific description of various types of stem, leaves, flowers, buds, hairs, thorns, and prickles lies beyond the parameters of this book. For further information, a book on basic botany is recommended. For suggested titles, refer to the Bibliography.

STEMS

Initially observe the particular shape of the stem girth, and then the direction in which it grows. Long sweeping lines, such as the edge of a long stem, are generally composed of a series of shorter lines. These are easier to draw and are joined together to form the impression of one length of continuous line. If parallel lines are difficult to achieve, it is simpler to draw the whole length of one side of a stem first. When this has been established, add the opposite side to complete the stem. The width of the stem may be usefully marked out with pencil reference marks, or a dotted line, before the length is drawn.

When installing a length of stem, observe where it connects to any visible calyx or petiole, and the location of leaf scars and buds. At this point, ridges, ribbing and textures, as well other markings, may require delineation. Make short pencil marks to denote where the leaves connect to the stem, or where the leaves conceal the stem. When the stem disappears behind a leaf or leaves, ensure that it reappears in the appropriate place.

LEAVES

Observe the manner in which leaves connect to the stem and how they are individually formed. Generally, leaves are arranged in patterns around the stem, and each individual leaf or set of leaves displays characteristic shapes and growth patterns. Determine these arrangements and observe precisely what is occurring, by looking around the stem and viewing it from all angles.

When drawing each leaf, it is often appropriate and less complicated to construct the midrib first, and build the shape of the leaf around it. This procedure assists in the construction of a symmetrical leaf and the correct appearance of a foreshortened leaf in perspective. Foreshortened leaves, and those that twist and turn, must display a midrib that moves naturally through the upper and lower sides of the leaf in a continuous way.

If the edge of a leaf is serrated or wavy, construct the edge as a single pencil line, before adding the serrations and waves, or indicating any thickness of the leaf that may be apparent. Finally, draw the veining pattern by detailing the principal veins, followed by the smaller veins. Ensure that the veins end at the appropriate places within the leaf area. Always construct the larger leaves first and then build the smaller leaves around them. Leaves commonly overlap. It is necessary to check that, as each leaf reappears from behind another, it does so in the correct location.

FLOWERS AND THE REPRODUCTIVE ELEMENTS

Initially, it is necessary to make certain that a drawing of a flower is assembled so that it sits naturally upon its stem or pedicel, and appears connected to the plant when the stem is not in view. Also, observe how the petals emerge from the calyx, and the position of the teeth of the calyx in relation to the petals. For petals that display ruffles, crimping, or fringing on the margins, first indicate the overall shape with a single outline. Thereafter, add the characteristics. Figure 11 shows the outline of the petals and sepals of *Canna* 'Wyoming', before the ruffling was included.

The plant's sexual parts require very careful observation in order to appear naturalistic. A group of stamens and a pistil must be in the right proportion to the petals in which they are nestling. Therefore, always count the number of stamens when it is practical to do so. When drawing a large number of stamens, or a cluster of small stamens, first outline the shape that they form collectively, and then divide this whole shape into sections. Observe and draw the stamens, in each appropriate section, until the whole group becomes installed within the flower.

As a flower unfolds, the anthers will begin to change shape, colour, and texture as they open to reveal the pollen. Observe these changes and draw the collection of anthers at the same time, so they all exhibit the appropriate stage of development in relation to one another.

The veining in petals may be clearly visible, as well as any ridges, waves, textures, and colour patterns. Indicate these details after the whole petal shape has been constructed.

BUDS

Each flower bud has a clearly visible calyx that may well disappear from view when the flower opens, unless it is seen from the back or possibly the side. Observe the direction that the bud faces and ensure that it is drawn in an appropriate size for its stage of growth. Buds develop and expand and all are characterised by their shape and volume. This is formed by their compacted contents of leaf, stem or flower. In a well-developed flower bud, it is often possible to observe the lines where the calyx will soon separate to reveal the flower petals. The comportment or bearing that a flower displays, as it begins to unfold from a bud, explains a great deal about the individual character of a plant. If buds are changing

quickly, it is often practical to draw and paint them first. When other areas require attention, it may be necessary to adjust the drawing of a bud to accommodate any minor changes.

HAIRS, THORNS AND PRICKLES

If hairs, thorns and prickles are present and visible, they must be included as part of the drawing. Observe the places that these are located, their arrangements, their size and their density. If a surface has a downy covering made from tiny soft hairs, it is best to describe them as an overall texture. The drawing can mark the extent to which a particular area is covered, and the rest may be more appropriately defined through dry brush painting. Single white hairs or thin prickles may be drawn with a single pencil line that can be left unpainted. Indicate the thickness of each hair by the thickness of the pencil line. Paint around these, and erase the lines when the painting is complete, leaving a white space to represent the hair. Thorns and prickles both terminate in sharp points, and it is important to define the direction in which they grow away from the plant surface. In addition, the length and sharpness of the point requires clear definition.

14 Composition

Rules

Composition is the art of arranging parts to form a unified whole. This simple definition brings with it a legacy of rules and principles. Many of the recommendations that prevail are by no means essential to the creation of a beautiful work that is in sympathy with the plant. It is more important to let the plant be your guide to a natural arrangement. It is always obvious if a composition has been carelessly thrown together or if the artist has run out of picture space. Beyond these obvious inadequacies, many arrangements are pleasing to the eye. The solution to the problem of how to produce an interesting and satisfactory composition lies fundamentally in the creation of unity. This, as we shall see, occurs when various elements work in harmony with one another to create a balanced arrangement.

Selection

You may wish to include the whole of a plant in a painting, or choose to focus on a particular area. To arrive at a decision, begin by looking at the plant whilst turning it and holding it at different angles before your eyes. Observe with an open mind and with the intention of absorbing as much information as possible about the specific and individual character of the plant. Plants display flowers, stems, and leaves at different stages of growth, offering a comprehensive account of their life cycle. Note the manner in which a flower opens, or a leaf expands or unfurls, and the direction the stems take as they grow outwards into space. The changes that occur as a flower opens are a source of real fascination, and, when incorporated into a composition, they offer a valuable pictorial link between the buds and the full bloom.

The viewpoint

Every point of view reveals something different about the plant. A straightforward side view of a flower and stem with the flower on the eye level produces a good classical arrangement. All plants offer some kind of perspective, and the more complex compositions incorporate this into the work. The view taken in Figure 12 of *Lilium longliflorum* 'Ice Queen' shows the long trumpet shapes of the blooms in perspective, moving from the foreground into the background.

Perspective views offer an infinite range of possibilities for a composition, because the relationships between the component parts of a plant always appear to change whenever the artist's point of view changes. A cluster of flowers growing from the branch of a tall tree has a particular appearance if observed directly from beneath. This same cluster will look very different when cut from the tree and placed squarely in front of one's eyes.

Difficult views are often avoided because the angles that need to be understood and drawn out seem too complex. The illusion of looking up to or down at a plant may actually appear more natural, and it is sometimes the case that a flower reveals its most interesting features when seen in perspective. To ensure a correct interpretation, it is essential to distinguish very clearly what lines point upward and what lines point downward. Artists tend to become associated with particular types of viewpoint, and often produce their best work by painting what they know best and love most. Nevertheless, to specialise in a particular style of composition that comes from habitually seeing only one type of view may become restrictive.

Right 12 *Lilium longiflorum* 'Ice Queen'
(size:760 x 570mm)

Form and negative space

A naturalistic flower painting floats in a field of white paper and there is no background. The unpainted area surrounding an image is known as negative space. The painted image is responsible for creating the shapes and sizes of all the negative space that exists around it, and the two elements interlock to form a cohesive whole. Before composing a picture, observe the shapes and sizes of the negative space existing between the flowers, leaves and stem. Consider how these will sit around the image and how they will compliment it as part of a painting. Negative space brings balance when combined with an image because the white paper is regarded as a real space, instead of simply a flat white surface. The use of negative space is largely intuitive, and there are no absolute rules, but the best way to become aware of its effect is to observe it. Most spectators will not be aware of a good use of a negative space in a flower painting, but will sense and appreciate the feeling of unity that it brings.

The paper edge

The intentional use of negative space influences the size of paper needed for a picture, as well as the selection of either a square or rectangular format in which to place the plant. Depending on its structure, a plant can enter into the picture via any part of the paper's edge, including the top or sides. Seeing the composition as a window, through which only a section of the plant is seen, is particularly effective for large plants such as *Delphinium* 'Faust' in Part II. Cutting an image with the edge of the paper works well if the composition holds the eye's attention firmly within the picture.

When the edge of the paper cuts a bloom in half, the arrangement will appear unified only if the rest of the composition contains other prominent full blooms.

Movement and rest

To understand the notion of movement and rest it is useful to view the plant as an abstract form by analysing it into straight lines, diagonal lines, and curves. Lines and shapes that echo the edge of a piece of paper and run parallel to it are generally static. Curvilinear and serpentine shapes, diagonal lines, spirals, and circles are all dynamic shapes that prompt some eye movement. The shapes made by the negative space around the leaves and flowers can encourage the eye to move on to the next image or to rest after absorbing information about the plant. The painting of the *Lilium longiflorum* 'Ice Queen' (Figure 12), originated from two lily stems grown in a large pot. One was curving across the other, providing the opportunity for a compositional link between the two plants. The curved stem leads the eye upward from the bottom of the page to the circular arrangement of buds and flowers.

The focal point

The most prominent part of a plant often becomes the focal point of a painting. A composition can lead the eye to this point, by means of a diagonal line or negative space that points towards it. Even so, the strongest accent in a flower painting is just as likely to be a small spot showing an intensely bright highlight, or an area of colour or tonal contrast. A definite focal point is useful to a composition, but by no means essential.

Stems

Stems are sometimes difficult to place, particularly when only part of a plant is included in a composition. Some artists favour fading the end of a stem into nothing in the middle of space. This works well in large pictures, when the faded part is located away from the main areas of interest. In smaller works (less than A1 in size) faded stems are distracting to the spectator, who often loses faith in the illusion of realism on seeing this. Painting a stem as cut, with space around it, is a more purposeful arrangement. A stem cut at an angle, as in Figure 12, can reveal the internal structure of the stem, providing an additional dimension to the painting.

15 The Thumbnail Sketch

THE PURPOSE OF THE THUMBNAIL SKETCH

Produced in rapid succession, little thumbnail sketches explore possible compositional arrangements. Each one is a small, speedy pencil study of a plant, positioned within a square or rectangle, which represents the edge of the picture. The task of putting a composition together presents a complex puzzle, and this method of sketching enables us to reject ideas that prove unsuitable in favour of one that works well.

THE VIEWFINDER

A viewfinder is a small piece of card that has a rectangular or square window cut from it. This is held up between the eye and the plant subject. It frames a view of the plant and isolates it from surrounding details and distractions.

It is useful to create several of these little devices of differing proportions, with which to the view a plant before a thumbnail sketch is drawn out.

To create a series of basic viewfinders take four pieces of stiff card 15 x 20cm (6 x 8in approx) in size.
On one of the pieces, draw and cut out a square, size 7 x 7cm (2³/4 in x 2³/4 in). On the remaining three of the pieces draw and cut out a series of rectangles in sizes:
  7 x 9cm (2³/4 x 3¹/2 in)
  7 x 11.5 cm (2³/4 x 4¹/2 in)
  7 x 14cm (2³/4 x 5¹/2 in)
Use a strong ruler and a sharp craft knife or blade to cut the card.

THE THUMBNAIL SKETCH METHOD

To produce two simple thumbnail sketches, first draw a square size 7 x 7cm (2³/4 x 2³/4 in) and a rectangle size 7 x 9cm (2³/4 x 3¹/2 in), with an HB pencil, into a sketchbook, or onto cartridge or graph paper. The window of a viewfinder can also provide a handy template for a drawing of a box for a thumbnail sketch. Produce one of these by placing the viewfinder card flat onto the sketching paper and drawing around the window with a pencil.

Thereafter, experiment with a composition by simply choosing a view of a plant and placing a sketch of it in one of the small boxes with an HB pencil. From here on, experiment to find the most suitable arrangement. Draw boxes of assorted proportions, and sketch different views of the plant within these boxes, continuing until the most appropriate arrangement develops. The *Tulipa* cultivar, Figure 13, shows the thumbnail sketches that were produced for the simple composition of the pink tulip in Part II. Sketches 'a' and 'b' were combined to produce the arrangement for Figure 12, *Lilium longiflorum* 'Ice Queen'.

Figure a

Figure b

13 *Tulipa* cultivar
Thumbnail sketches

16 Light and the Tonal Sketch

THE PURPOSE OF THE TONAL SKETCH

The term 'tonal' refers to the general effects of light and shade, and 'tonal evaluation' is the process of discerning the relative values of light and shade. An awareness of both of these factors is essential if we are to create a flower image that has volume and appears naturally solid. By using monochrome (black and grey) only, the tonal sketch helps us to acquire sensitivity towards the light and shade that is part of our plant. From this we can more readily understand the tonal pitch of its colour.

ILLUMINATION

A plant's relationship to its light source requires careful consideration, as lack of attention to this detail may deprive the painting of its realism. When light flows over a plant directly from one side, as described in Chapter 5, it depicts the form and surface texture in a combination of highlights, mid-tones and shades. If a plant is too far from the light, it appears to lack volume, through the absence of highlights. If a plant is too close to the light, there may be too much contrast between light and shade, and the lack of mid-tones will render it insubstantial. The distance required varies with the size and structure of the plant. When utilising natural light from a window, arrange the plant and yourself in relation to the light. If using a lamp, adjust it to suit the plant and yourself.

REFLECTED LIGHT

This type of light appears on the plant form as a very low level highlight, and is only observable on an area of the plant that would otherwise be in shadow. Reflected light originates from a light coloured object with a smooth surface. This bounces light back from a main light source, and shines it onto the plant. Generally, this is not as bright as a light from the principal light source. For a flower painting, the most suitable surface for creating reflected light across the whole of one side of a plant is a white piece of card, or a white wall, opposite the window. To cast bright reflected light, use a strong piece of card, the same height and width as the plant, and fold back two opposite edges, so that it will stand up right. Place it on the side of the plant that is farthest from the main light source, and face it directly towards the light. In these circumstances, light emanates from the main light source, reflects from the white card, and shines onto the shadow side of the plant. When there is no reflected light present, the areas in darkest shade appear on the parts of the plant that are farthest from the main light source. When reflected light is included, the darkest tonal area on the plant moves toward the centre of the form. This is because the subdued highlight, produced from the reflected light, is on the side of the plant that would normally be in shadow.

This reflected light effect is obvious on smooth curved forms such as stems, giving them a heightened sense of solidity and roundness. This is distinct in Figure 14, a preliminary Tonal Sketch of a pink tulip, made before the colour painting of the same flower, shown in Part II. If a plant has a naturally dark coloured stem, this may contrast with the whiteness of the paper, causing the dark edge to appear to move towards the eye, and create the impression of a concave stem. This can be offset by the inclusion of reflected light, which also throws into relief the surface textures, such as the veining systems and other distinguishing marks that may be obscured through lack of light.

lighter

lighter

Primary
Light
Source

Highlight

Reflected
Light

Shaddow

14 *Tulipa* cultivar
Tonal Sketch

Transluscent

another

lighter

lighter.

lighter.

reflected light

lighter.

Transparent

CSS '99

reflected light

reflected light.

15 *Canna* 'Wyoming'
Tonal Sketch

Utilising the tonal sketch

Learning to look at a plant tonally, rather than in colour, may initially be an uncomfortable concept. But, with regular practice, perceiving the form of a plant this way becomes an automatic process. It can be useful to imagine you are seeing the plant as a black-and-white film or photograph. In addition, look at a plant with half closed eyes to simplify the form. A tonal sketch functions as an information gathering process that uses very rapid brush strokes, and has an informal quality. It may be as simple or complex as you feel is necessary. It may be a small area of the plant, such as a leaf or flower, or the whole image contained in a composition sketch. On some occasions, a few brush marks will suffice, at other times a succession of sketches and annotation is required to accrue the right amount of understanding.

Figure 14 is a relatively simple statement, and includes errors in the highlighted areas. It is easy enough to lose highlights, and this sketch provided knowledge of the problems waiting to be encountered in the final colour painting. A tonal scale, such as that placed alongside the tulip, assists evaluation of the tonal range, and can be held beside the plant for reference. To produce this scale, apply rich neutral tint paint to a damp piece of paper, with a Nº 6 brush. Grade this with water to create the tonal changes. On many occasions, comparing the plant with a strip of paper painted with a black or neutral tint, or with a black object, is a more accurate way of assessing the true value of a tone.

For tonal sketches, always work on pieces of watercolour paper or watercolour sketch blocks, using larger rather than smaller pieces of paper. This allows enough space around your sketch for any later additions and information. Avoid tiny sketchbooks as these will narrow your vision and inhibit your hand movements.

The tonal sketch method

The neutral tint mixture, as described in Chapter 11, is the only paint mixture required for the tonal sketch. This produces a dense black, which contrasts with the brightest highlights produced by the white of the paper. When diluted with water, this mixture produces all the grey mid-tones, from the palest to the darkest, that range between the black and white. Ready-made black paint, and the watercolour manufactured and labelled as 'neutral tint' are also suitable for monochrome sketching. These have a slightly different depth and colouration to the one described in this book, and are worth experimenting with if you wish to save time when sketching by using ready mixed paint.

Before starting the sketch, dilute the neutral tint with water to create three tones of grey wash. These are light grey; mid-grey; and dark grey. This will provide a resource of the three basic tones.

Begin the work by sketching out the plant, with an HB pencil.

Figure 15, the sketch of *Canna* 'Wyoming', was used to gauge the subtle differences in tone seen within the group of orange flowers. Sections of the plant were painted individually, beginning with the largest petals, and working toward the smallest areas. The light grey wash was applied first, on damp paper, using a Nº5 and Nº6 brush.. This corresponds to the areas on the plant that are slightly darker than the brightest highlights. This pale tone was graded into the brightest highlights, which were left unpainted. Thereafter, a Nº5 brush was used to repeat this process across the rest of the plant, using the mid grey from the palette. This was applied to match that level of tone observed in the plant. Finally, the third and darkest grey from the palette was applied. This represents the darker areas of shade in the plant. All tones were blended together during the process. Whilst the paint was still damp, a Nº3 brush was used to apply venation to the flowers.

When dry, the third mid-tone was overlaid, on the stem and other areas, to create a fourth very dark tone, which was close to black. Finally, some small touches of rich neutral tint were added to the darkest areas of the stem, to create the blackest shades. This process secured many tones of grey between the polarities of white and black, to establish the full tonal range contained in the plant. Beside the main image, notation was also included. For some plants, it may also be beneficial to use some dry brush work to explore various textures or minutiae.

17 The Colour Study Method

THE PURPOSE OF THE COLOUR STUDY

The colour study is a watercolour sketch that functions as a testing ground for colour mixtures and painting methods. These are set out in a freely painted and annotated form. As preliminary work, the colour study resolves any difficulties that may otherwise arise during the painting of a detailed picture, such as those in Part II of this book. It is a rewarding process, which is no less interesting to produce than the more highly finished flower painting. For artists who incline towards working in a loose style, the colour study method is an end in itself.

DEFINING THE HUE

The first task is to analyse the fundamental hues contained within the plant. The appearance of every hue is altered by excessive light, or by lack of light, but each one requires initial definition before the effect of any of these light factors may be analysed.

For the sake of continuity, we shall turn our attention to Figure 18 (page 67), the colour study of *Canna* 'Wyoming', that we have already observed in tone. The plant was lightly sketched out on watercolour paper, using an HB pencil, allowing space around it for additional information. The brightly coloured raceme displays many closely related hues that differ subtly in terms of saturation and relative warmth and coolness (see Chapters 9 & 12).

The basic hue present in each part of the plant was evaluated by observing it in good flat day light, away from excessive sunlight or deep shade. When using artificial light, avoid intense spot lighting when assessing a hue. These were analysed before any painting work on the pencil drawing took place. These were mixed and stored on the palette as mixtures. Colour blocks of the basic range of orange

hues found in the flowers were placed to the upper left of the sketch. Each orange hue is composed of cadmium lemon and cadmium red. Some of the warmer hues of orange are biased toward cadmium red, and some of the relatively cooler hues of orange lean towards cadmium lemon. Colour blocks of the stem and stalk hues are to the lower right, and include permanent magenta and neutral tint. During this process, the paper was held close to the plant, and the hue mixtures were compared with those of the plant. As an alternative, if a spare plant subject is available, it is useful to remove a petal and leaf, and place this against the colour study, to help gauge the right colour mixtures.

In addition to the basic hue of the petals, a more highly saturated deep red/orange hue was apparent amidst the enclosure of flowers. Many blooms, particularly roses, display this characteristic deepening of hue that is not endemic, but which occurs when reflected colour bounces back and forth between closely grouped petals.

DEFINING THE TINTS AND SHADES

There are always parts of a plant where the hue overpowers the tone and appears 'true', requiring no adjustment. All the tonal differences seen in the plant can relate to the parts where the hue is authentic, and not affected by excessive light or shade. The tonal sketch has already assisted our understanding of form, and through the colour study our perception of colour and tone begin to merge. We follow this through by observing and mixing the tints and shades of the basic hues found in the plant. In Figure 18, the basic hues present in the plant were diluted in the usual way to create the tints. For the shades, neutral tint was added. This addition of varying dilutions and different amounts of neutral tint

16 *Paeonia lactiflora* 'Sir Edward Elgar'
Colour Study

cloudy

Single
(herbaceous)

Pen rose
Qui Hay

cadmium
white.

pale
tint.

17 *Paeonia lactiflora* 'Sir Edward Elgar'
Colour Study

completed a full range of tonal hues. A degree of transparency was present in the petals and sepals of the *Canna* 'Wyoming', forming part of the lightest areas of colour tone. Colour blocks of these mixtures were placed to the upper and lower right of the sketch. The annotation surrounding the blocks includes a description of the mixtures and additional information. At this stage of the work, always note and record any distinguishing surface textures, surface bloom and surface shine.

COMBINING COLOURS AND PAINTING TECHNIQUES

At the end of this first part of the process, there was a series of colour blocks and written notes on the paper, as well as a series of colour mixtures on the palette, providing all the information needed to paint the sketch. Through painting the sketch, we accrue an understanding of what combinations of colour and technique, and how many layers of paint, are necessary to achieve the most naturalistic effect. If you feel unsure precisely what techniques to use, or in what order to use them, this is the time and place to experiment.

In Figure 18, the highlights and the visibly transparent aspects of the petals were laid down first, over the drawing, and onto damp paper. This was immediately blended into the mid-tone areas of petal, represented by the pure hue mixtures. Thereafter, the remaining shaded hues were blended into the pure hues, producing the areas of the plant located in shadow. The sketch was painted rapidly, with a Nº5 and a Nº6 brush, without concern for precision but with the intention to create an accurate impression. The flourish and bravado that is required to achieve this comes with practice. In some petals, there are two layers of paint, with the veining integrated between these. The stem was painted in two layers of paint, after establishing the petals. Watercolour paint soaks into the paper surface and dries to a paler colour than it appears to be when it is wet. To allow for this and to save time, the colour study generally uses slightly richer paint than that used for a highly finished work.

COLOUR PERCEPTION

Our perception of one colour alters in relation to the colour that is next to it. Pale cream flowers generally appear white when viewed alone or against dark green leaves, but, when laid against white paper, they are seen as having a colour. This tells us that our perception of colour is relative. Complementary colours are those considered to be entirely opposite each other, and when mixed together they cancel out each other's colour value, producing grey or neutral brown tones. Therefore, a complementary colour is occasionally suitable for reducing the colour strength of its opposite pair. The most common complementary pairs are magenta or red & green, blue & orange, and violet & yellow. The green of leaves particularly affects magenta and red flowers which, owing to their complementary nature, appear brighter together than when seen separately. The human eye is said to be constantly producing subtle adjustments in colour perception, in order to relieve colour saturation. With practice, we may become sensitive to these changes and make allowances for them when mixing colour. These optical adaptations are particularly prevalent when looking at brightly coloured flowers surrounded by leaves. When juxtaposed, these bright colours generally appear to be in greater contrast, and therefore more dissimilar.

COLOUR PERSPECTIVE

It is generally true that any contrasting elements in a picture appear to move forward, and any closely related colours or tones remain static or seem to recede. If we compare the colours of the nearest leaves of a plant to any that are at a distance, we find that those farthest away appear cooler and paler. On close inspection, the farthest leaves show themselves to be composed of a number of hues which merge in the distance. This is evident when a perspective view of a plant shows a group of leaves receding away from the foreground. It is beneficial, therefore, to stand back from a colour study and look at it to see if the colour perspective visible in the plant is working in accordance with the composition.

Cad lemon
+
Cad Red.

venation

Burnt
Hue

Tilted
scale

Covering

red red
reflected
vein

anthers

Permanent
Shaded
Hue

18 *Canna* 'Wyoming'
Colour Study

Stem

Veronica longifolia

PART II

Flowers through the Spectrum

Lilium longiflorum 'Mount Everest'
Family *Liliaceae*

 *The Lilium longiflorum, or long-flowered lily is native to the subtropical islands of Japan, and many named forms have been cultivated, with blooms in differing quantities and stems of varying heights. During the 19th Century, millions of bulbs were imported each year from Japan, and forced into bloom for the spring-time florist trade. It has since been known as the Easter lily. All varieties have the characteristic long tapering blooms with waxy, white 'petals', golden stamens, and intense perfume. There are six 'petals', technically known as perianth segments or tepals, and six stamens. The cultivar 'Mount Everest' produces up to ten glistening flowers in summer, from a mature bulb. This young plant produced four blooms in its second year of flowering, and is available from specialist growers. Many similar cultivars are available from flower shops throughout the year.*

THE SPECIMEN:
A cut flower stem, grown from a bulb and flowering in June, and secured in Oasis set within a low glass vase, with a wide circumference.

THE LIGHT SOURCE:
Daylight, from a north-facing window, was located to the upper left of the flower stem. Reflected light was not present, avoiding the inclusion of too many light tone areas.

THE COLOUR PALETTE:
Cadmium lemon
Cadmium yellow
Cadmium red
Cerulean blue
French ultramarine
Neutral tint

THE COMPOSITION:
The plant displays both bud and bloom, viewed slightly from above, and all facing in the general direction of the light. The stem is located to the right of the arrangement to provide a strong vertical element. The green leaves act as a foil for the open white bloom. These rich green leaves define some of the lightest edges of the pure white flower, which shows little colour or tone. The image is cut to the right of the stem, to increase the 'window' effect of the composition.

THE DRAWING:
Initially, the boundary edge of the whole composition was marked out. The central open bloom was established first, using a viewfinder and a plumb line. The buds and half-open bloom were included, using the 'clock-face' method to define the angles of the perianth segments, and a window-viewfinder to assess the curves. The stem and leaves were added, with attention to the correct perspective in each leaf. Finally, the reproductive elements of the main bloom and all the venation were drawn out. The drawing was lifted with a kneaded eraser to lighten the image in preparation for the watercolour.

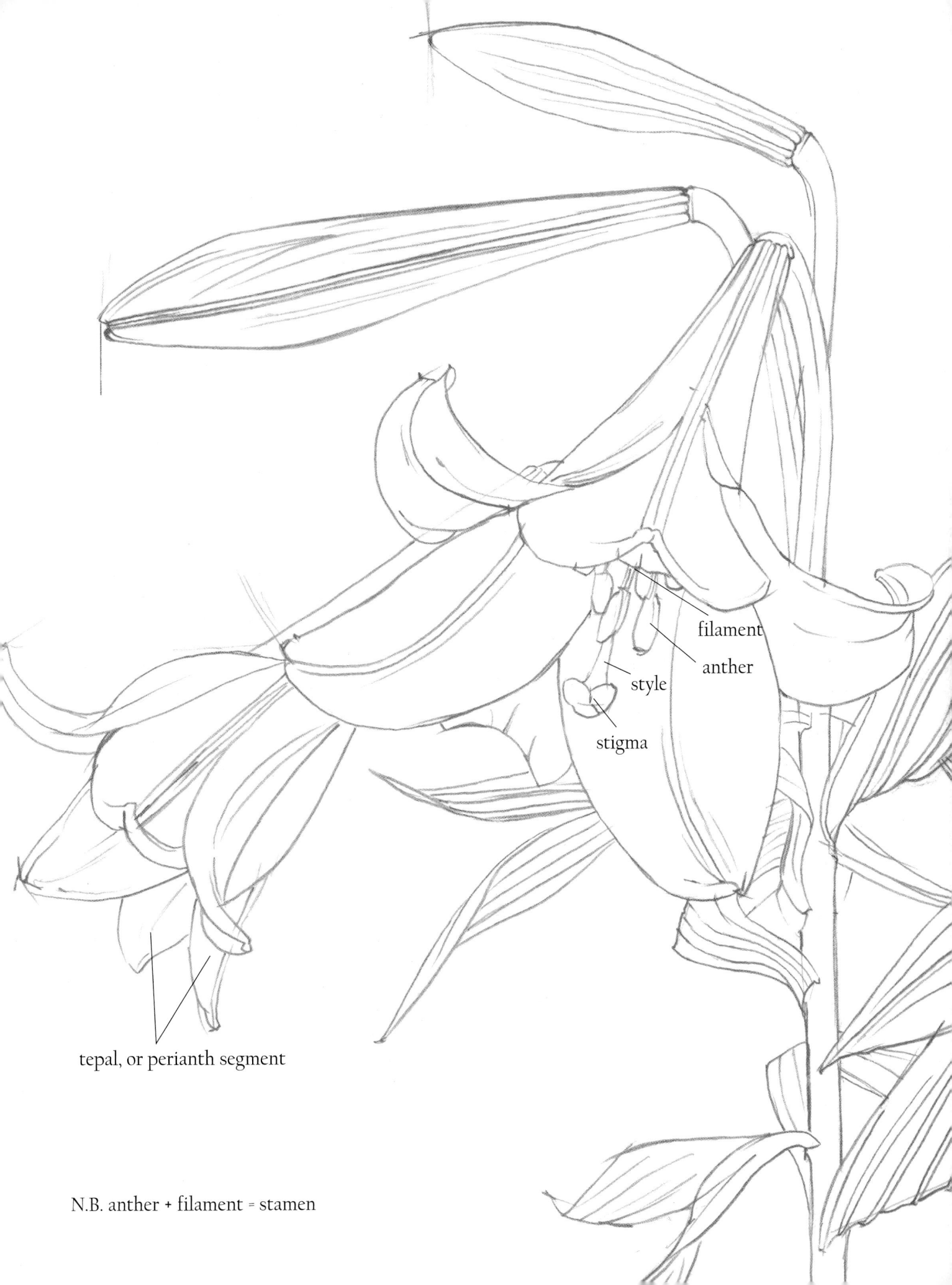

filament

anther

style

stigma

tepal, or perianth segment

N.B. anther + filament = stamen

1. The half-open bloom: all layers

The half-opened bloom on the left was in a rapid process of change and needed attention at the beginning of the work. At this stage, the flower displays colour that is mid-way between that of the bud and full bloom. The perianth segments are a dull greenish yellow made from cadmium yellow and neutral tint, with a touch of cerulean blue. The less saturated colours in shadow contain more neutral tint. A N°5 brush was used to apply the flat washes onto damp paper. The subtle colour gradations were blended and graded towards the highlights. The bloom was painted rapidly, using two layers of paint in the shaded parts.

2. The buds and flower stalks: first layers

The shadow areas of the largest bud were painted first, and were made of the same colour combination as used for the half-opened bloom, with the addition of more cerulean blue. Using a Nº5 brush, onto damp paper, the shadows were defined and graded into the light. On the smaller bud, a Nº3 brush provided for greater accuracy. A sweeping dry brush created the surface texture of both buds, using a Nº5 and Nº3 brush, respectively. The junction of each bud with its stalk was painted with a slightly darker green combination. This included the addition of cadmium lemon, French ultramarine and neutral tint. A flat wash was applied, with a Nº3 brush, onto damp paper. This was graded into the lightest areas.

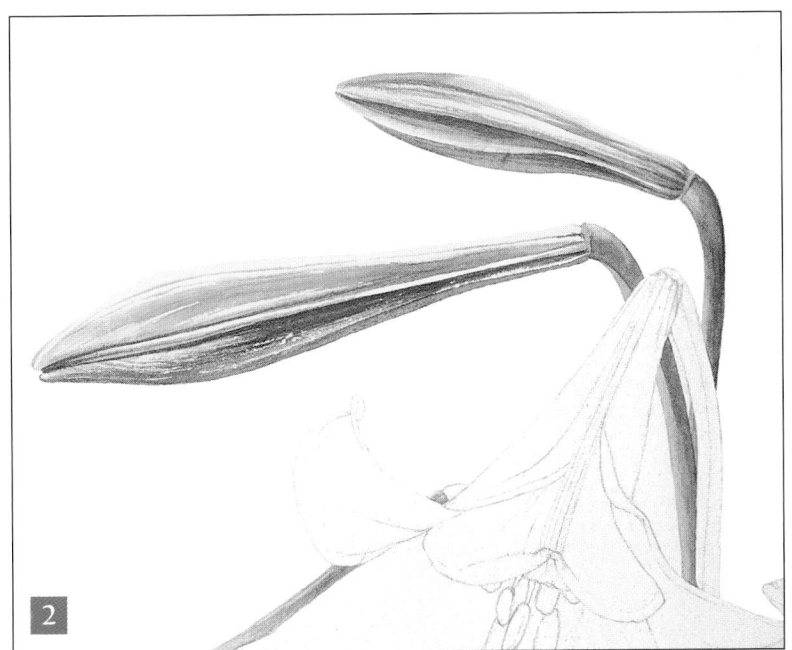

3. The buds and open bloom: the final layers of the buds, and the first layers of the open bloom

The shadows were deepened, using the same colour as in the first layers. The buds were completed, with the addition of some bright green wash made from cerulean blue and cadmium yellow, on the upper part of the larger bud, and the whole of the smaller bud. The same sizes of brush were used as in stage 2 and the techniques were repeated, but painted onto dry paper. The outer surfaces of the perianth segments of the main bloom were painted in the same way as the half-open bloom.

4

4. The open bloom, leaves and stem: the first layers

Since the drawing, some subtle changes had occurred in the curves of the open bloom and the arrangement of the reproductive elements. These were adjusted, before the painting work began.

The first layers of the perianth segments were painted with Nº5 and Nº3 brushes onto damp paper. For the palest edges of the bloom, a neutral tint mixture was used, to which some cerulean blue was added. A flat wash of this colour was graded to the whitest parts, which required no paint, thus achieving a translucent quality. The greenish throat, which is mainly reflected and shaded colour, used a combination of cadmium lemon, cerulean blue and neutral tint. The filaments were this same green, with the addition of more cerulean blue. The anthers were also in shadow, but in these first layers, the bright orange/yellow was painted.

This was a mixture of cadmium yellow and cadmium red, shaded with neutral tint. The style was painted with a mixture of cadmium lemon, cerulean blue and neutral tint. A Nº 1 and a Nº3 brush was used for these elements, which were painted onto damp paper using a combination of flat, blended and graded washes.

The stem and leaves were painted to the same level as the flower stalks in stage 2, using a mixture of green, but varying it towards yellow or blue, to create a variety of warm and cool greens. The stem was painted in sections, and the leaves one at a time, working from the top downwards, using a Nº3 and a Nº5 brush, onto damp paper.

5. The open bloom, the leaves, stem and flower stalks: the final layers

At this stage, the parts painted in stage 4 were repeated and strengthened with more paint, to emphasis the shadows and highlights. The same brushes and techniques were employed, and, in addition, the same colour mixtures were used. The subtle combinations of warm and cool, and light and dark, particularly in the leaves, stem and flower stalks, were emphasised. More neutral tint was added to the basic hue colour present in the anthers, filaments and style, to shade the area, and reduce the colour. The shadows on the white bloom were overpainted onto dry paper, and care was taken not to lose the bright white areas that were left unpainted.

5

Anemone coronaria 'The Admiral'

(Saint Brigid Group)

Family *Ranunculaceae*

 *The anemone takes its name from the Greek anemos, the wind, and mone, a habitation, hence its common name, the windflower. Pliny wrote ' the flower hath the property to open when the wind doth blow', but, contrary to this name, Anemone coronaria does not enjoy cold wind but flourishes in the gentle warm breezes of the Mediterranean. Saint Brigid Group is a collective name for a race of double-flowered cultivars of this species. 'The Admiral' bears large, solitary, semi-double flowers of a rich violet-mauve. Each flower is encircled by finely divided bracts and held on a stiff, twisted stem. The plant produces its flowers naturally from late spring to early summer, but this and many similar Anemone cultivars are available from flower shops for much of the year.*

THE SPECIMEN:
A potted plant, grown from a corm and flowering in May.

THE LIGHT SOURCES:
Daylight from a north-facing window, situated to the upper left of the plant, produced a range of tones from highlight to shadow. A moderate amount of reflected light, from the white wall opposite the window, was absorbed by the right side of the stem.

THE COLOUR PALETTE:
Winsor violet
Permanent magenta
Cerulean blue
French ultramarine
Cadmium lemon
Neutral tint

THE COMPOSITION:
This particular bloom was just beginning to unfurl, and was chosen for this reason. The composition shows a view of the stem that reveals this change occurring. The flower is located centrally on the page, to balance the curves present in the stem, bract and flower. The flower is displayed very slightly below eye level.

THE DRAWING:
The basic shape of the bloom was drawn by measuring the proportion of one part against another. The angles of the leaves and stem were included, using the 'clock-face' method. These parts were related proportionally to the bloom. The overlap of the segments on the left of the bloom was drawn. The venation on the segments and the leaves was then included. Finally, the ridges along the tubular stem were outlined. The drawing was lifted with a kneaded eraser, to lighten the image in preparation for the watercolour.

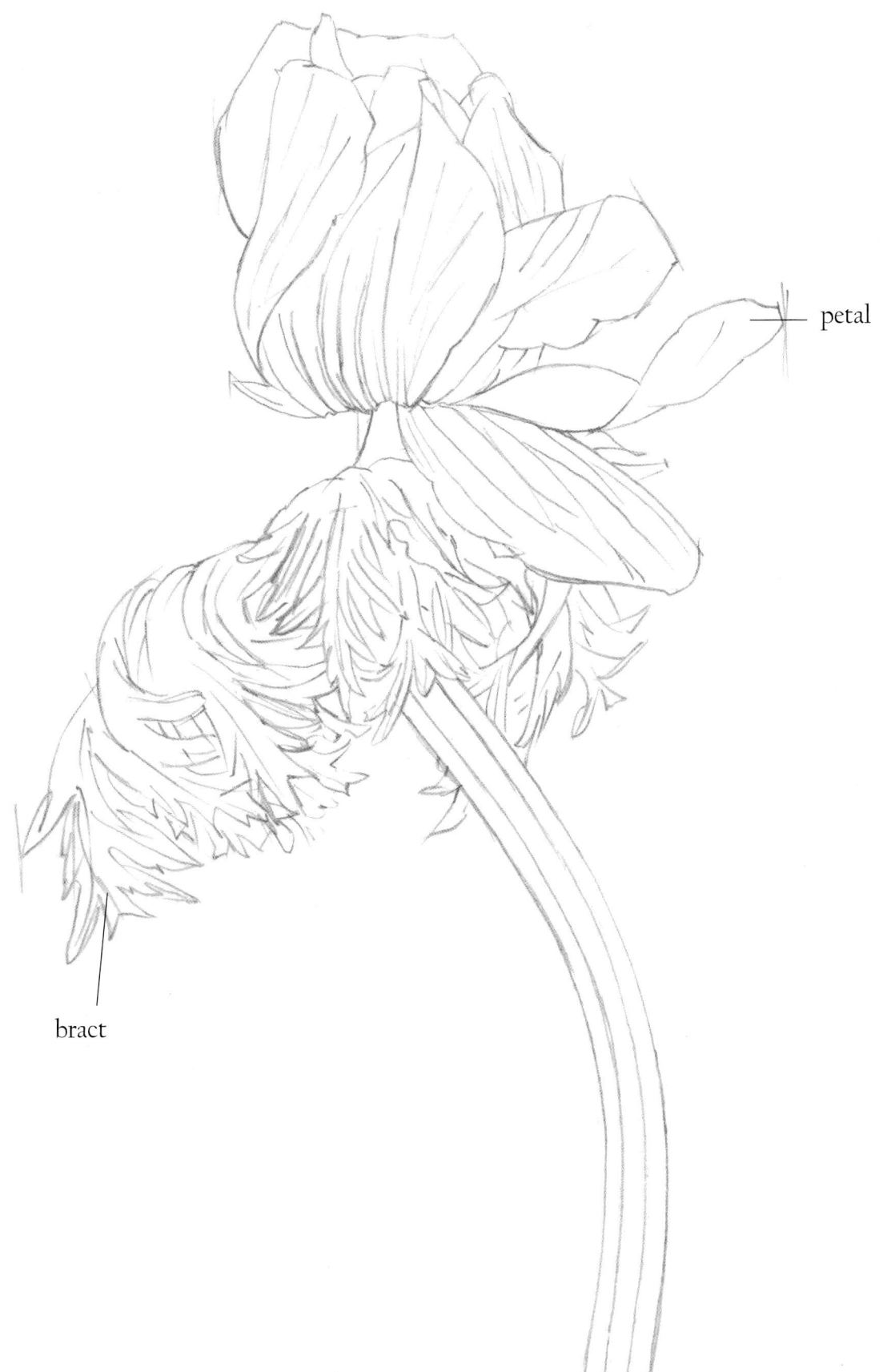

petal

bract

1. The flower: first layers of shadow

The inside of the bloom was in shadow, and these segments show the deepest colour of the anemone. They were painted with a mixture of Winsor violet and neutral tint, which produced a cool, shaded violet. The outside of the unopened flower bud, that displays underside of the segments, is a paler tint of the same basic hue colour. This was applied as a thin wash, and, graded into the highlights. Each segment was painted individually, with flat and blended washes, using a Nº 5 brush, onto damp paper. Some veining was drawn in, with a Nº1 brush.

2. The flower: first layers of tint

The palest segments were added to the painting with a colour mixture containing mostly Winsor violet and a touch of neutral tint, using the same techniques as in stage 1. These lightest parts of the flower were painted with a very thin dilute wash, applied to damp paper, and leaving the brightest areas unpainted. The more neutralised shaded tones, found in the shadows of the overlapping segments, were also included.

3. The flower: last layers of shadow

The stage 1 process was repeated, but onto dry paper. Some veining was drawn out with a Nº1 brush. The colour of the shaded segments and the opened segment on the right side of the flower were intensified with the addition of a cerulean blue and permanent magenta. This was overlaid, creating subtle changes in the warmth and coolness of the basic violet hue of the flower.

4. The flower: last layers of tint

The stage 2 process was repeated, but onto dry paper. The venation was emphasised with a Nº1 brush.

5. The flower: enriching the colour

The highlights created in stages 2 and 4 were overlaid in part with a mixture of Winsor violet and permanent magenta to add more warmth. In part, these were overlaid with a mixture of cerulean blue and Winsor violet to add richness. Some brighter highlights, seen on the veins, were left unpainted. All washes were laid onto dry paper using a Nº5 brush.

6

6. The bracts and stem: the first layers of shadow

The shaded areas of the bracts and stem were all painted first, using green hues, composed of varied amounts of French ultramarine, cadmium lemon and neutral tint. Winsor violet was used to reduce the saturation of this green and harmonise it with the violet of the bloom. A bright green made from French ultramarine and cadmium lemon was displayed along the ribbing, located on the left side of the stem, next to the highlight. All watercolour was applied onto damp paper with a Nº5 brush, using a flat wash that was graded and blended in parts.

7. The bracts and stem: enriching and modelling

A further mixture of cadmium lemon, French ultramarine and Winsor violet was painted over the stem to enrich the colour. Some neutral tint was added to this, to create the shaded part of the stem below the bracts. These flat and graded washes were laid onto dry paper, using a Nº5 brush. This area was modified to accommodate the minute changes that had occurred since the original drawing. The upper side of the bracts were modelled with a Nº3 brush, onto dry paper, using a mid-green, made from cadmium lemon, French ultramarine, and a little neutral tint. This was biased towards yellow in some areas and towards blue in others. The modelling was painted in sections, working from left to right, and was overlaid to build the depth of colour. Some venation was delineated with a Nº1 brush during this modelling process. The greyish highlights were painted with a very dilute wash mixture, made from French ultramarine and neutral tint. This was blended into the green colours to create a continuous surface of changing colour and light.

7

Delphinium elatum 'Faust'

(Elatum Group)

Family Ranunculaceae

 *The name delphinium is derived from the Greek word for little dolphin – each flower possesses a spur, thought to resemble a dolphin's head. The Elatum Group comprises those varieties most commonly cultivated as garden perennials. The term elatum, meaning tall, refers to the flower spike, the cultivar 'Faust' growing to about 1.5 metres in height. The flowers are a rich ultramarine colour, produced by an anthocyanin pigment. The individual flowers on the flower spike are often known as florets, and the 'petals' are actually sepals. As in many double or semi-double flowers, the central, smaller 'petals' are in fact modified stamens (staminodes), surrounding a cluster of anthers.*

THE SPECIMEN:
A potted herbaceous perennial, grown from a cutting and flowering in July.

THE LIGHT SOURCES:
The plant pot was placed on the studio floor, beside a north-facing window, situated to the upper left of the plant. Each floret cast a slight shadow onto the one below, throwing the whole inflorescence into relief. A substantial amount of reflected light was absorbed from the white wall opposite the window.

THE COLOUR PALETTE:
French ultramarine
Cerulean blue
Winsor violet
Cadmium lemon
Quinacridone magenta
Yellow ochre
Neutral tint

THE COMPOSITION:
The composition shows a section of the upper part of the acropetal spike. The sense of scale is emphasised by cutting the image at the top and bottom edges of the page. The eye level is situated below the centre of the composition. This emphasises the height of the spike.

THE DRAWING:
Initially, the whole form was outlined as a block. The upper flower stalks (pedicels) were added first, and a system of squares and rectangles was used to gauge the placement of the flowers. The edge of each open flower was marked out, and the basic outline drawing was lightened with a kneaded eraser. The petals and their venation on the florets was detailed directly before each section was painted.

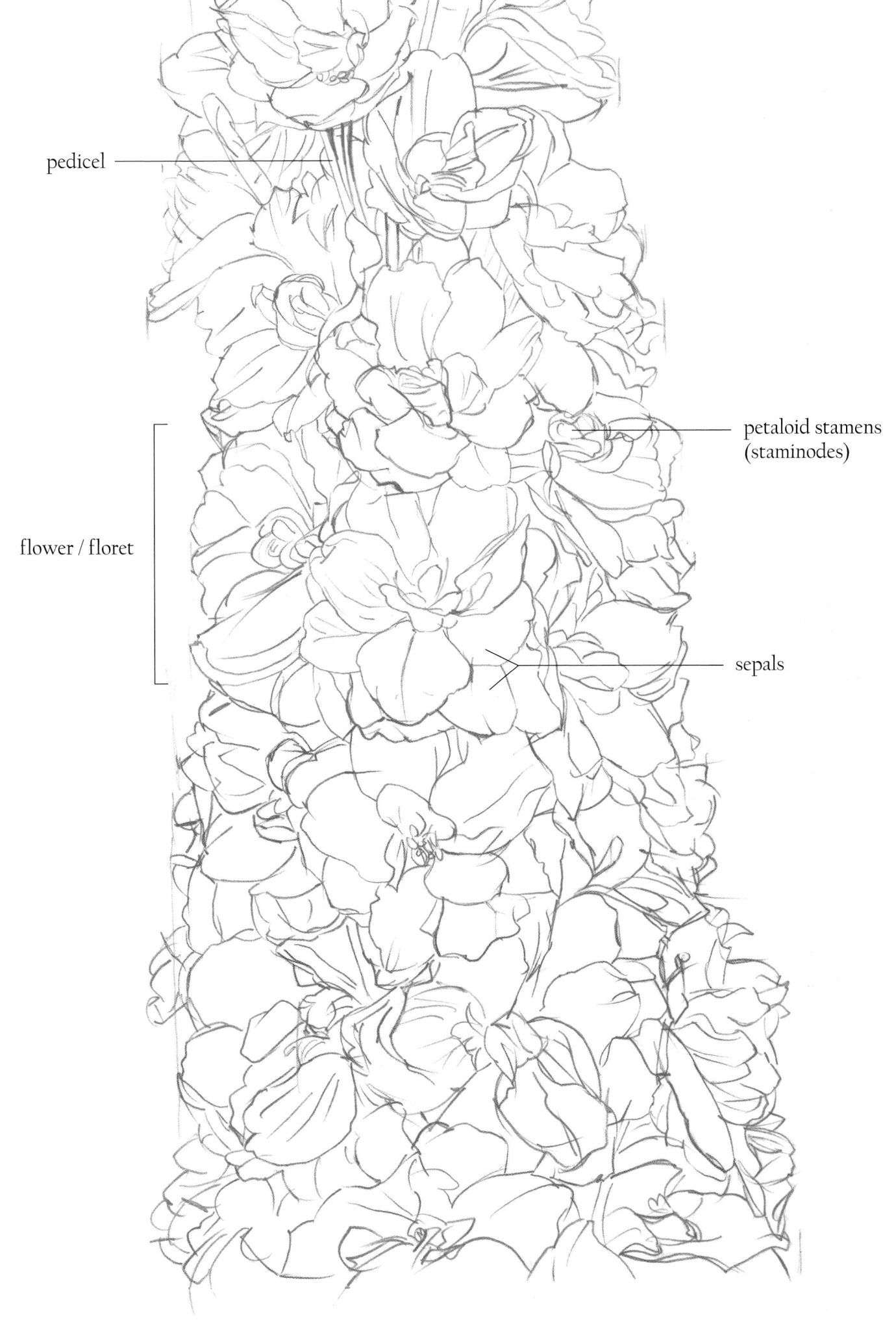

pedicel

petaloid stamens
(staminodes)

flower / floret

sepals

1-3. The florets: first layers of blue

The first part of the process involved assessing the underlying basic blue hue found in the florets. This was analysed as a combination of French ultramarine, Winsor violet and neutral tint. The flower spike was painted in stages with this mixture, working from the top downwards. Using a Nº5 brush onto damp paper, flat and graded washes were employed. In addition, some variations of the basic blue hue were included and laid down using a graded wash: Cooler variations were made by adding a little more Winsor violet to the basic hue. Adding cerulean blue to the basic hue made warmer variations. Some neutral shades of blue were made by adding extra neutral tint to the basic hue. This reduced the colour saturation.

3

4-5. The pedicels and the florets: layers of green, and enriching the colours and highlights

The pedicels were largely in shadow and painted with two layers of green mixed from French ultramarine, cadmium lemon and neutral tint. Some quinacridone magenta was added to this mixture for the areas imbued with a pinkish hue. Each pedicel was painted with a Nº3 brush, on damp paper, using a blended wash to connect the different shades of green.

Continuing with a Nº5 brush, onto dry paper, the highlights on the florets were overlaid with a wash of pale Winsor violet.

The inner 'petals' were imbued with a deep indigo colour, made from neutral tint and a touch of French ultramarine. Between the edges of these 'petals', some of the stamens were visible. These were a dull yellowish hue, made from yellow ochre and neutral tint. Some yellow ochre hue also imbued the edges of the inner 'petals'. The inner 'petals' and the stamens were painted with a Nº3 brush, onto dry paper.

At this stage, the whole image appears somewhat flattened, but enriched with colour.

5

6. The florets: the final layers of shading

The final layers of wash were applied to deepen the overall tone of the flower shadows, creating a voluminous image. The angles at which the sepals point outward into space is understood from their shape in perspective, and the depth of the shadow that they cast. Some are at a more obtuse angle than others, and catch more light because of this.

Working from the top downwards, onto dry paper, each shadow area was made denser, using a mixture made from cerulean blue, French ultramarine and neutral tint.

A Nº5 brush was used for painting this colour in flat and graded washes, on dry paper. A Nº5 brush was also used to indicate the surface textures of the sepals. For this, the sweeping dry brush technique was applied to dry paper using a mixture of quinacridone magenta and Winsor violet. In addition, some veining was drawn with a Nº3 brush. At this stage, some minute changes in the appearance of the sepals were apparent, which were included using a Nº3 brush.

6

Fritillaria imperialis 'Lutea'
Family *Liliaceae*

 *The Latin fritillus, meaning dice box, refers to the small Fritillaria meleagris, whose tepals are chequered like a chessboard, once associated with games of dice. Its larger more majestic cousin Fritillaria imperialis was introduced into Europe in 1576. Indigenous to the deciduous woodland of Iran and Turkey, the yellow cultivar Fritillaria imperialis 'Lutea', bears a circle of lemon-yellow, bell-shaped flowers, crowned by a mass of green, leaf-like bracts that protect the flower head from the rain. The stigmas protrude below the rim of each corolla, and the pendulous arrangement of the flower shields the reproductive parts until fertilisation has taken place. As with all fritillaries, the base of each of the six 'petals' (technically known as tepals, or perianth segments) possesses a tiny globule of liquid nectar, which nestles within a cavity. The plant, which emanates a strong fox-like odour, bears its flowers at the top of a tall stem, well above the glossy, lance-shaped leaves.*

THE SPECIMEN:
A potted plant, grown from a bulb and flowering in April.

THE LIGHT SOURCES:
Daylight, from a north-facing window, was located to the upper left of the plant. Reflected light was included, from a piece of white card, placed to the right of the plant.

THE COLOUR PALETTE:
Cadmium yellow
Cadmium lemon
French ultramarine
Cerulean blue
Raw umber
Neutral tint

THE COMPOSITION:
The plant displays the crowning bracts and the newly opened flowers, seen slightly from below to reveal the styles and stamens. The flower head is located to the centre of the page, slightly off-setting the stem to the right. The leaf appearing on the lower right was the only one to reach this height, and its presence indicates the existence of leaves on the lower part of the stem.

THE DRAWING:
The group of bracts and ring of flowers were marked out in rectangles and squares, and the basic shapes of the bracts and flowers were drawn within these blocks. The stem and lower leaf were then added. Following this, the bracts were outlined. The styles and stamens were defined, and the veining of the petals was indicated. Finally, the ridges of the stem were included. The drawing was lifted with a kneaded eraser to lighten the image in preparation for the watercolour.

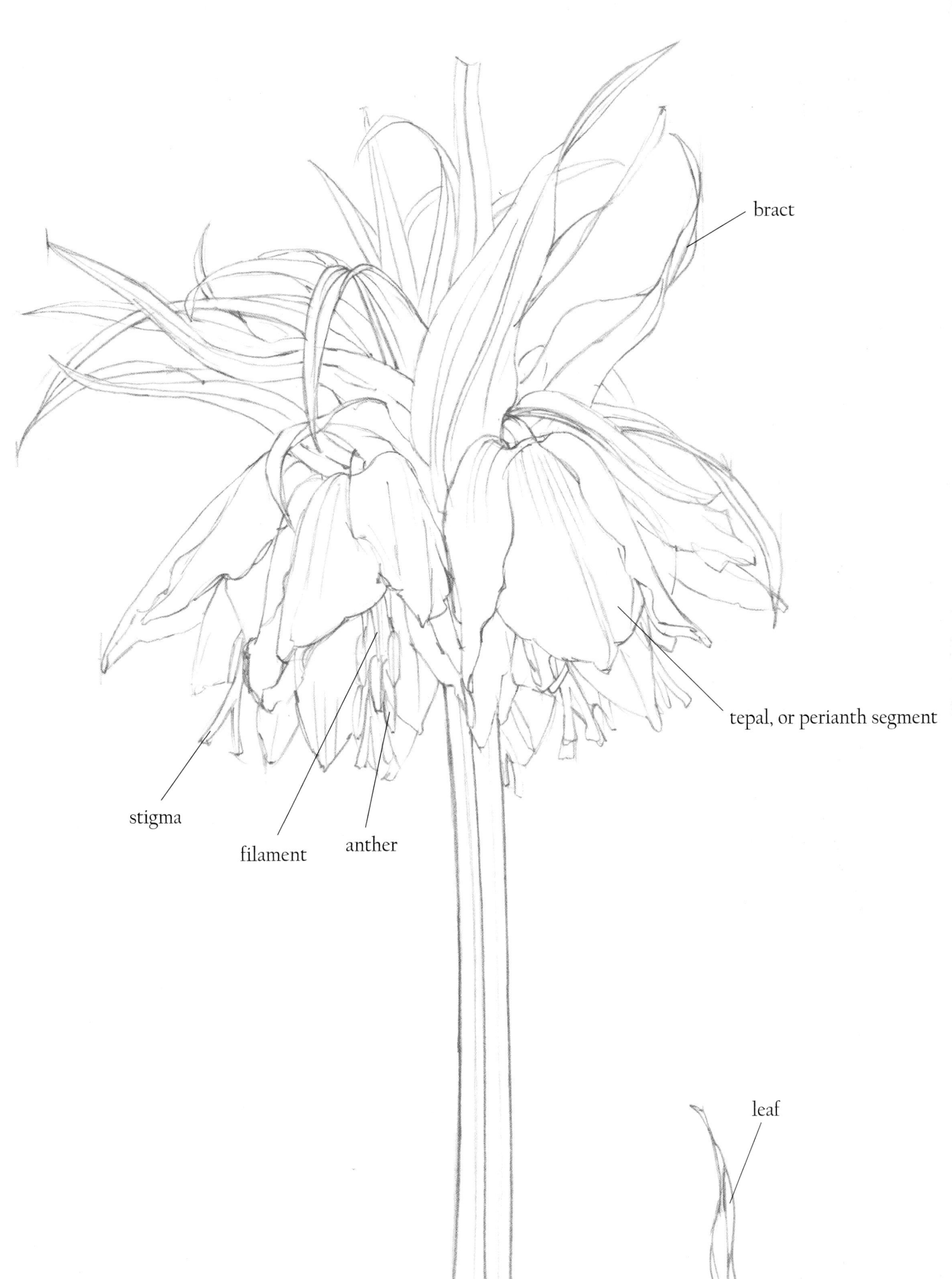

bract

tepal, or perianth segment

stigma

filament

anther

leaf

1. The flowers: first layers of shaded yellow

As yellow is the lightest colour of the spectrum, it is generally preferable to paint the darkest shadows first to establish the form. The basic hue of the flowers is a mixture of cadmium yellow and cadmium lemon. Neutral tint was added to this to create the shaded areas. Adding more cadmium yellow to the mixture produced the warmer areas of shade. These colours were painted onto damp paper, with a Nº5 brush, and graded into the highlights. The main veins on the outside of the flowers were left unpainted. The colour of the greenish vein lines, situated at the base of the petals, was made from French ultramarine and cadmium yellow. These were drawn over the shaded paint, with a Nº3 brush, on dry paper.

2. The 'petals' and reproductive parts: enriching the colour and defining the detail

Each 'petal' was entirely overlaid with a flat wash of the basic hue, using a Nº5 brush, on dry paper.

The anthers were painted with a mixture of neutral tint, raw umber and cadmium lemon, using a Nº3 brush on dry paper. Some of the deeper coloured details of the anthers were drawn with a Nº1 brush, using the same colour, with some more neutral tint added. The filaments were shaded with neutral tint, using a Nº1 brush on dry paper.

The upper part of the style showed a greenish tint, which was made from French ultramarine and cadmium lemon.

3. The reproductive parts and the bracts: finishing the detail and the basic green hues

The tones and colours of the reproductive elements in stage 2 were repeated. In addition, the anthers and filaments were imbued with a yellow reflected from the flower bells.

Each leaf-like bract was painted with a mixture of cadmium yellow, French ultramarine, cerulean blue, and neutral tint. This hue mixture was varied towards neutral tint in the shaded areas, towards cadmium yellow in the warmer areas, and towards French ultramarine in the coolest areas. The palest tints were nearest to the highlight or in the distance. These were made from a dilute wash of cooler green. The brightest highlights remained unpainted. A Nº5 brush was used on damp paper, apart from the highlight on the central bract, which was painted onto dry paper with a sweeping brush technique. The bracts farthest away were painted first.

4

4. The stem and lower leaf: first layers of green
The first layers of the lower leaf were painted with the same basic green hues used on the bracts, using a Nº3 brush, on damp paper. A mixture of cadmium yellow, cerulean blue, French ultramarine and neutral tint was used for the basic hue of the stem. The shadow areas were laid first and graded into the highlight, using a Nº5 brush on damp paper. (See stage 5 for the lower leaf.)

5. The bracts, stem and lower leaf: final layers of green
The stage 3 painting of the bracts was repeated to deepen and intensify the colour and tone. The edges of the brightest highlights were covered with a very dilute wash of cerulean blue and neutral tint, using a Nº3 brush, on damp paper. This activates a highlight by making the unpainted areas of the paper appear a more brilliant white.

Stage 4 was repeated to achieve the necessary depth of colour and tone. When dry, the stem was overlaid again with the basic green, using a Nº5 brush using short sweeping dry brush strokes to achieve the grainy pigmentation. The stage 4 painting of the lower leaf was repeated.

94

Canna 'Wyoming'
Family *Cannaceae*

 *The name Canna is derived from the Latin cana meaning, meaning cane or reed. The family Cannaceae contains only one genus, but many cultivars are in existence, producing brightly coloured, tropical looking flowers on tall spikes. They are native to the open forest areas of tropical South America. Valued for municipal planting, the 'Indian Shot' is also favoured for its contribution of hot colouring to the summer border. Canna 'Wyoming' has a raceme of extraordinarily bright orange flowers that are produced in pairs from the axil of each bract. Each flower is asymmetric, with three petals and three sepals, but the conspicuous large coloured parts are in fact modified stamens (staminodes), one of which bears a single anther.*

THE SPECIMEN:
A potted plant grown from a rhizome, flowering in September.

THE LIGHT SOURCES:
Daylight, from a north-facing window, was located to the upper left of the plant. Reflected light was created by a piece of white card placed to the right side of the stem. The card was the same height as the stem.

THE COLOUR PALETTE:
Cadmium lemon
Cadmium red
Permanent magenta
Neutral tint

THE COMPOSITION:
The composition shows two racemes at different stages of development. One is open and in full bloom and the other is closed. These were existing side by side as part of the same plant. The flowering raceme fits squarely onto the page, as a life-size image, with the inflorescence on eye level.

THE DRAWING:
The boundaries of the form were marked out first. The shape of each individual flower was established with the use of a plumb line (see Chapter 13). Thereafter, the bracts, stem, and bud were placed into the arrangement. The final inclusions were details of the petal veining and the tips of stamens, which were visible in some flowers. The drawing was lifted with a kneaded eraser to lighten the image in preparation for the watercolour.

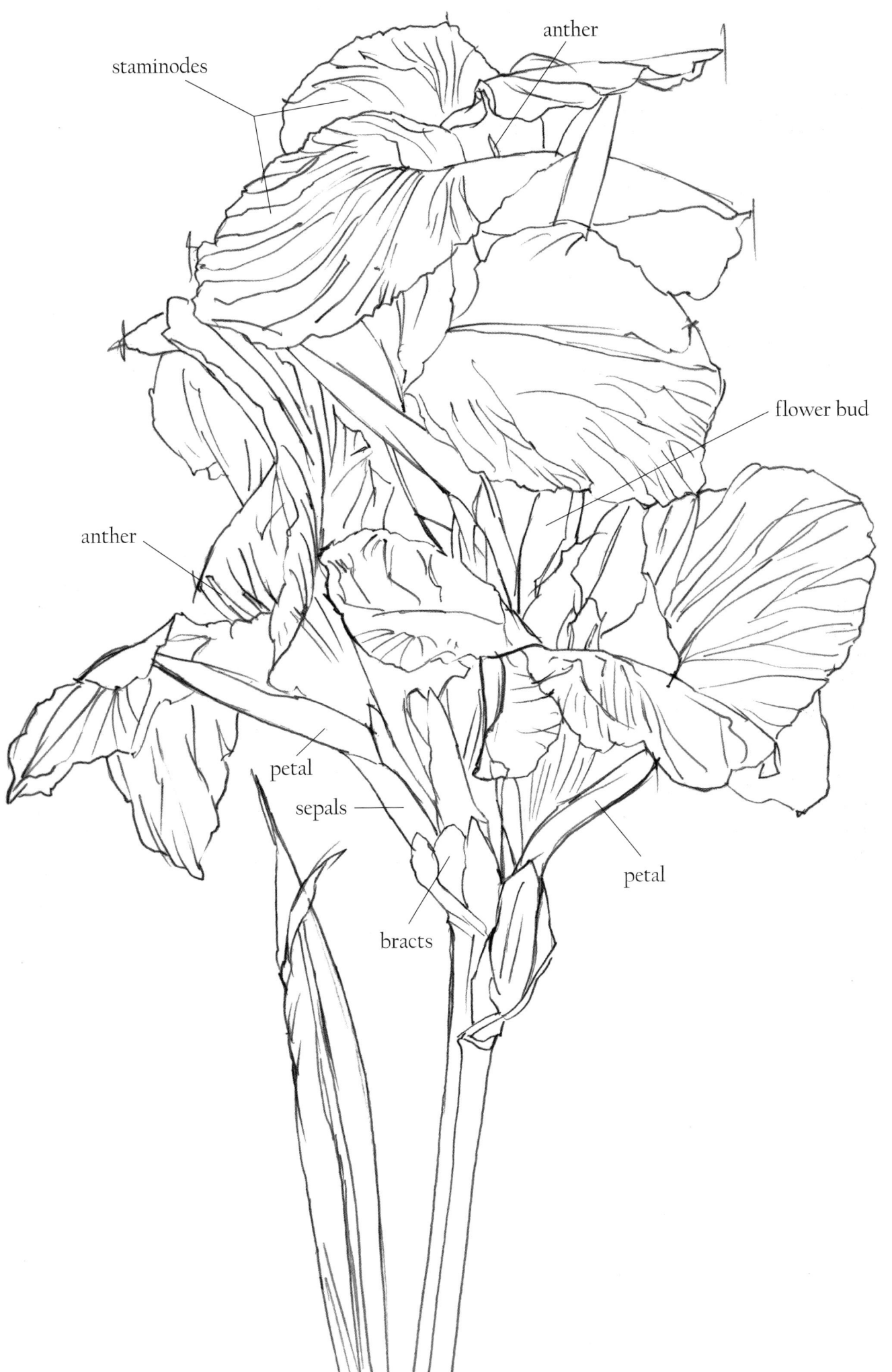

1

1. The staminodes: the lightest tints and the transparency

The basic hue of the staminodes consisted of cadmium lemon and cadmium red. This hue was diluted to produce the tints. Some of the tints were warmer and biased towards red, and some were cooler and biased towards orange/yellow. For some colour areas, where a neutralised orange was needed, the neutral tint mixture was added to reduce the saturation of the basic hue. The highlighted areas of the flowers, and the parts displaying the characteristic transparent texture, were painted with the tint mixture, onto damp paper with a Nº5 and Nº6 brush. These were graded to the light, where necessary, to ease the connection with the next colour. Whilst still damp, a Nº3 brush was used to draw the venation. The damp paper caused the brush drawing to soften and correspond with the plant's characteristic veining.

2. The staminodes: the basic hue and the mid-tones

The variety of mid-tone areas were blended into the tints, on damp paper, using the same brushes as in stage 1. These ranged from hot reddish hues to warm orange hues, some of which were reduced in saturation by the addition of a little neutral tint. The venation was drawn within these areas, using the deeper hues.

3. The staminodes: the reflected colour and the shades

The colour of the shaded areas of the staminodes was made from the basic hue mixed with neutral tint, completing the tonal range with a selection of brown hues. These were applied to damp paper, and were graded into those painted in stages 1 and 2. The rich red/orange of the reflected colour, seen within the flower arrangement, was overlaid on dry paper, to enrich the colour intensity. The venation in the staminodes was deepened, where necessary, to correspond with the richer tones now included in the painting.

4

4. The bracts, buds, and stem: the first layers

These parts complete the structure of the raceme, and are mainly composed of a basic hue mixed from permanent magenta and neutral tint. The warmer hues were biased towards a magenta/brownish hue, and the cooler were biased towards a deep greyish/brown hue. The area was painted in these colours, onto damp paper with a Nº5 and a Nº3 brush. The washes were graded to the highlights, which were left unpainted to establish the form. In the darkest areas, two layers of paint were applied, with the second onto dry paper. The petals at the base of each flower were imbued with an orange hue, which was produced by adding the magenta mixture to the basic hue of the flowers. In addition, some pale pinkish tints were present in the highlighted areas. This was produced from pure permanent magenta. The solitary anthers were a cream colour, but were imbued with the reflected orange colour from the petals. The shading on the anthers was drawn with a Nº1 brush onto dry paper, using a mixture of neutral tint, cadmium lemon and a touch of permanent magenta. The anther on the far left flower cast a shadow onto the flower.

5. The bracts, buds, and stem: the final layers

The flower bud, located within the flower group on the right side of the arrangement, was overlaid with a hot orange hue, using a Nº3 brush, onto dry paper. Stage 4 of the process was repeated, to deepen and enrich the hues.

5

Camellia japonica 'Adolphe Audusson'
Family *Theaceae*

 *The Camellia was named after a Jesuit of Moravia, called Joseph Kemel, who travelled throughout Asia and the Far East. This flowering evergreen bush is common in much of Japan, Korea, Taiwan, and southern China. In the mid-18th Century, Lord Petrie first grew this 'Chinese Rose' in Essex and by 1792 the first named cultivars had found their way to Britain, via the East India Company. Today the official International Camellia Register lists over 2,000 cultivars. 'Adolphe Audusson' takes its name from the plant breeder who raised it in 1877. It has remained one of the most reliable and beauteous of the red cultivars, displaying masses of semi-double, often upright flowers with a rose coloured tint, occasional pale edges, and bright yellow stamens. Dark, rich green leaves embellish this shrub, which is known for its ability to flower in the cool temperatures of late winter.*

THE SPECIMEN:
A container-grown shrub, flowering in March.

THE LIGHT SOURCES:
Daylight, from a north-facing window, was located to the upper left of the plant. Reflected light, from a piece of white card, placed close to the plant brought some subdued light into what would otherwise be a dark complex of blooms, buds, stem and leaves.

THE COLOUR PALETTE:

Cadmium red	French ultramarine
Alizarin crimson	Cerulean blue
Permanent rose	Raw umber
Cadmium lemon	Neutral tint

THE COMPOSITION:
The composition shows a section of the plant with blooms in various stages of flowering. The main open bloom, as the focus of the arrangement, is seen three-quarter from the front and located to the left of the picture, on the eye level. This appears to move forward towards the observer, whilst the other half-opened flowers sit in the middle ground, and the leaves break up the surrounding space. A section of the woody stem is shown; however, the internal structure of the stem is not seen in the picture.

THE DRAWING:
Initially, the boundary edges of the whole image were marked on the paper. The basic outline of the blooms and buds was included, using a window-viewfinder to establish their relationship to one another. A grid-viewfinder was used to find the perspective shapes of the leaves, and proportion the widths in relation to the lengths. The buds were added and the sepals were drawn around both of the half-open flowers. Thereafter, the petals of the large open flower were arranged within the basic round shape. Following this, the serrations on the leaf margins, and some of the leaf veins were outlined. A drawn dry brush method (see Chapter 8) was used to delineate petal venation during the painting process. The drawing was lifted with a kneaded eraser to lighten the image in preparation for the watercolour.

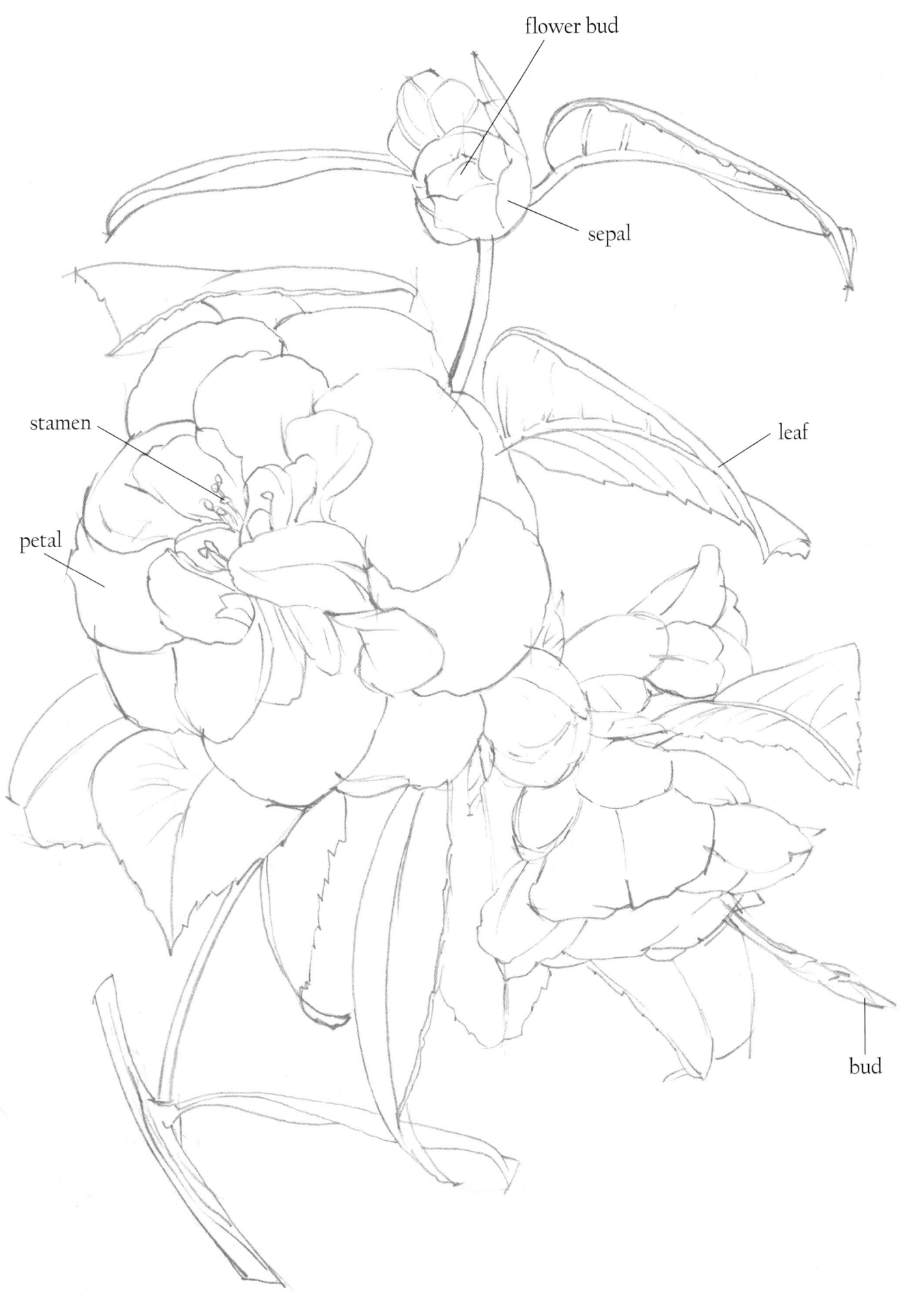

flower bud

sepal

leaf

stamen

petal

bud

1. The petals: the first layers, of warm and shaded hues, and the venation

The petals of the open flower, the half-open flower, and the largest bud, were all painted with a basic hue mixture of cadmium red and alizarin crimson. This was applied to damp paper, with a Nº5 brush and Nº3 brush, using a flat wash, which was graded towards the lighter areas. The venation was apparent on the edges of the petals catching the light, and was drawn with a Nº3 brush whilst the paper was still slightly damp. This layer included some of the dark areas of shade, in the recesses of the petals. Neutral tint was added to the basic hue to create the shaded hues. These were blended with the brighter reds. The smaller bud was not painted at this stage to allow for any alterations that might be needed as it began to open.

2. The petals and stamens: the second layers, of cooler pinkish hues, and some detail

The warm saturated red of the first layers was overlaid with a cooler mixture of permanent rose. This relative warmth and coolness of hue was combined to create the depth and range of colour required for these flowers. The pink was overlaid, with a Nº5 brush, onto dry paper, and was graded into the lighter areas, leaving some of the edges unpainted. The stamens were painted with a Nº1 brush, onto dry paper. The anthers were a mixture of mainly cadmium lemon, plus a little neutral tint. The translucent filaments were just visible, and painted with a very dilute wash of neutral tint plus a little cadmium lemon and cadmium red.

3

3. The small flower bud, terminal buds and the sepals: the first layers of bright green

Before any layers of green were applied, the drawing of the small flower bud was checked, and the red layers of compacted petals were painted, as in stages 1 and 2. The sepals and terminal green buds were painted in a mixture of cadmium lemon, French ultramarine, and raw umber. This was applied to each small section of terminal bud, with a Nº3 brush on dry paper. The colour was graded towards the light. The sepals displayed a velutinous texture, which was created with a modelling dry brush method (see Chapter 8), using the same green mixture.

4. The thin stems and the sepals: the first layers of rich brown, and final layers of bright green
The rich brown of the younger thin stems was made with a mixture of cadmium red, raw umber and neutral tint. These were painted with a flat wash onto damp paper, with a N°3 brush. These were blended into a paler, more dilute tint, to create the soft highlights, and the reflected light.

Stage 3 was repeated to develop the colour strength of these parts and to increase the sense of volume.

5. The leaves and woody stem: the first layers of dark and dull green, and the first layers of pale brown

The upper surface of the leaves was a neutral dark green hue, made from cadmium lemon, French ultramarine and neutral tint. This was applied as a flat wash, on damp paper. This was graded to the lightest parts, using a Nº5 brush. The undersides of the leaves were a dull, but rich green. This was made from cadmium lemon, French ultramarine, raw umber and neutral tint. This was applied as a flat wash, on damp paper. A Nº3 brush was used to paint each section between the main veins. These veins were left unpainted in the lightest areas, and the midrib was painted with a paler tint of the green. The lower woody stem colour was made from the same mixture as was used for the younger thin stems, with the extra addition of more neutral tint. This was diluted to produce the paler tint suitable for the older wood. This was painted with a Nº3 brush onto dry paper. The gnarled highlight of the surface was not painted.

6. The leaves, stems and flowers: the final layers of all the colours

The undersides of the leaves were completed, with the same hue mixture as in stage 5 which was biased towards a cooler green. A shaded hue was created with the addition of more neutral tint to the green. These were all blended on dry paper, using a Nº3 brush. The upper surfaces of the leaves were, overlaid with more dark green, onto dry paper. The highlights included some addition of cerulean blue to create the sheen, and the venation that was visible, was drawn over this with a Nº1 brush. At this stage, the other components required some deepening and an enriching of colour to balance them with the strong dark hues of the leaves. The edges of the petals were enriched with permanent rose. The lower stem colour was deepened slightly around the gnarled highlights, which were washed over with a dilute wash of cerulean blue and neutral tint.

Tulipa cultivar (unnamed florists' hybrid)
Family *Liliaceae*

 *The tulip takes its name from the Turkish work tulbend, meaning turban, which the flowers resemble. The bulbs were cultivated in Turkey for centuries before their arrival in Holland during the late 16th Century. The tulip has six 'petals', all of the same colour, technically termed the perianth segments, or tepals, and collectively they form the characteristic cup shape of the bloom. During early winter and spring, tulip hybrids are forced into flower en masse for the florist trade. Many modern hybrids now have the capacity to bloom more than once each year. Countless numbers of cultivars have come and gone over the years and some, such as this one, possess no name but simply a number allocated by the grower. This tulip was part of a bunch purchases as closed buds of pinkish green, which rapidly developed into ice pink blooms in the warmth of the studio.*

THE SPECIMEN:
A cut flower stem, from a bunch of florist's flowers, secured in Oasis, and set within a low glass vase with a wide circumference.

THE LIGHT SOURCES:
Daylight, from a north-facing window, was located to the upper left of the flower stem. Reflected light, created by a piece of white card, and placed to the right of the stem and bloom, emphasised their curved surfaces.

THE COLOUR PALETTE:
Permanent rose
Quinacridone magenta
Cadmium red
Cadmium lemon
Cerulean blue
Neutral tint

THE COMPOSITION:
This particular stem displays typical tulip characteristics, and the composition utilises the long curve of the fleshy stem and the long pointed leaf, to create a diagonal movement across the page. A slight shadow of the stem is cast across the leaf, bringing an additional dimension to the form. The placing of the bloom, just below eye-level, reveals the junction of the 'petals' and stem.

THE DRAWING:
The full length of the stem and flower was marked onto the paper, and divided proportionally into the flower, stem and leaf. The 'clock-face' method and a plumb line were used to establish the angles made by the stem and leaf. The left side of the stem was outlined first, and the right edge was drawn parallel to this, in short strokes that were connected to create the impression of one continuous line. The flower was divided proportionally into the 'petals' and the curves were gauged with the use of a window-viewfinder. Finally, a minimum amount of veining was delineated on both the flower and the leaf. The drawing was lifted with a kneaded eraser to lighten the image in preparation for the watercolour.

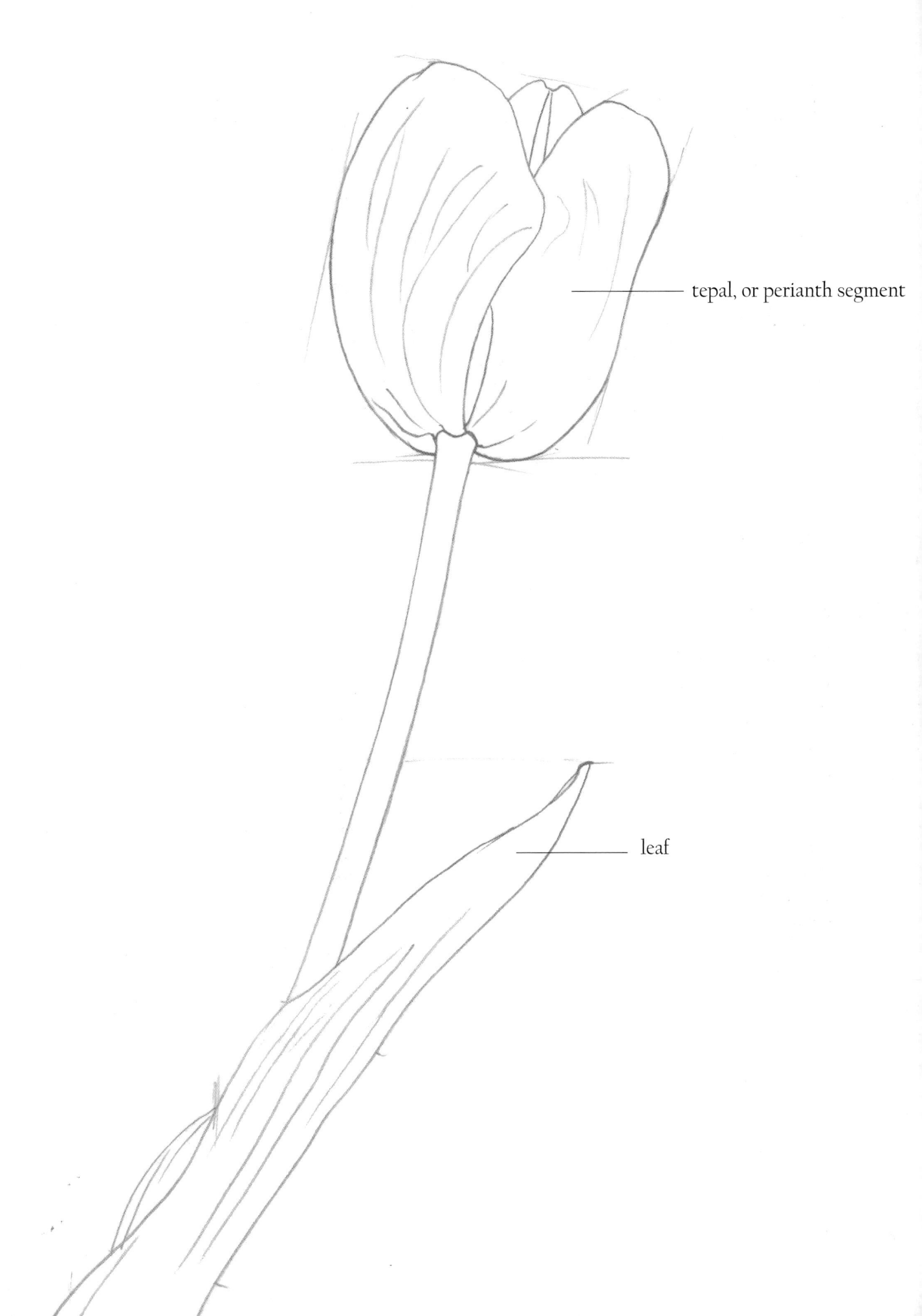

tepal, or perianth segment

leaf

1. The 'petals': the first layers of sweeping dry brush and blended colour

The basic pink hue of the 'petals' and was a mixture of permanent rose and quinacridone magenta, which had the saturation reduced with the addition of a little neutral tint. This was painted onto damp paper with a Nº5 brush, using a sweeping dry brush technique to denote the surface texture and venation. The highlights around this texture were left unpainted. The sweeping dry brush was blended with a flat wash of pink. These areas were then blended with shaded areas of pink, which were made by adding more neutral tint to the basic hue colour. At the base of the 'petals', a greenish tint occurred. For this hue, the shaded pink mix was added to a green made from cadmium lemon and cerulean blue. Each section was painted working from the top downwards, ensuring that the paper was damp enough to allow the washes to be blended.

2. The 'petals': the second layers of sweeping dry brush and blended colour

After drying, the first layers were made damp with clean water, and the stage 1 procedure was repeated to enrich and deepen the pink colour and the shaded areas. The distinction between the cool pink shadows and the warm pink hues was maintained.

3. The 'petals': the last layers of sweeping dry brush and blended colour

Stage 1 was repeated again, but this time it was on dry paper. Some very warm reflected pink was present in the centre of the flower. To achieve this, the basic pink hue was mixed with a little cadmium red, which was overlaid onto the existing cooler layers.

4. (Overleaf) The stem and leaf: the first layers of green

The basic hue of the stem and leaf was a combination of cadmium lemon, cerulean blue and neutral tint. The variations were warm yellowish greens and cool bluish greens, with shaded hues produced from the addition of more neutral tint. The stem was made damp along the central area, and a shaded mid-green wash was applied. This was blended towards the highlight on the left and the reflected light on the right. The leaf shadows were a cool shaded green, leaning towards cerulean blue and neutral tint. The brighter areas were a warmer, mid-tone of bright green. The two colours were applied to damp paper and blended together.

5. (Overleaf) The stem and leaf: the last layers of green

The left side of the stem was painted in a flat wash, on damp paper. This was made from a dilute mixture of cerulean blue and neutral tint to produce the cool highlight. The right side of the stem was also painted with a flat wash, on damp paper. This was made from cerulean blue, neutral tint and cadmium lemon to produce a warmer reflected light. The central area of the stem was overlaid with the same shadow green that was used in stage 4, also on damp paper. This darkened the shaded area, making the convex shape of the stem apparent.

The leaf was overlaid with some lines of shadow colour to denote the ribbed texture between the parallel veining. This was laid on dry paper. Further washes were applied over this when it was dry, using the same colours as in stage 4. These added further warm and cool greens to the leaf. A Nº5 brush was used throughout this stage.

5

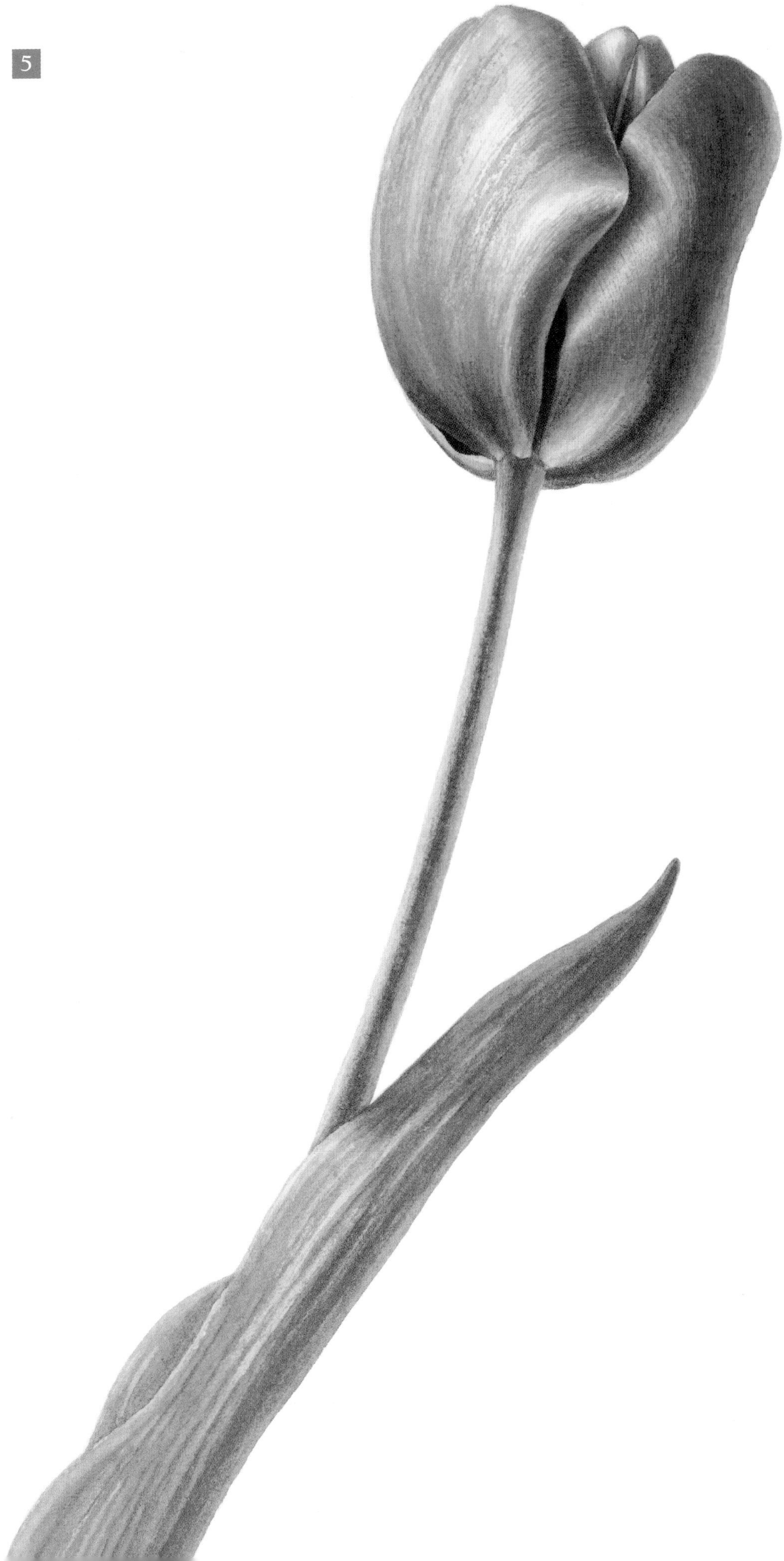

Strelitzia reginae
Family *Strelitziaceae*

 *Originating in the areas of Africa surrounding the Cape of Good Hope, the* Strelitzia reginae *first flowered in the Europe at the Royal Botanic Gardens, Kew. The species was dedicated to the reigning Queen, Charlotte, wife of King George III, who was from the House of Mecklenburg-Strelitz. A greenhouse plant in Europe, this so-called 'Bird of Paradise' provides exotic blooms for the florist trade. It has now naturalised across parts of Australia, where it enjoys much popularity as a garden plant. A crest is formed by the spadix as it emerges from the green spathe. The three sepals of brilliant orange are the first to appear, and these separate, to reveal three petals of pale violet-indigo. Two larger petals are formed together and contain the buff and brown coloured anthers. A third smaller petal conceals the ovaries and contains sweet-tasting nectar. Up to six flowers may appear in total, through the fissure along the top of the spathe.*

THE SPECIMEN:
Obtained as a cut flower from a florist, and set into Oasis, in a tall vase with a narrow circumference.

THE LIGHT SOURCES:
Daylight, from a north-facing window, was located to the upper left of the plant. A strong reflected light is apparent on the stem. This comes from a piece of white card, placed to the right of the stem to emphasis its volume.

THE COLOUR PALETTE:
Permanent rose	Raw umber
Cadmium yellow	Cerulean blue
Cadmium lemon	Cadmium red
Neutral tint	Winsor violet
French ultramarine	

THE COMPOSITION:
The horizontal format of the page frames the long pointed shape of the spathe. In addition, a side view on eye level was necessary to fully describe the complex arrangement of parts emerging from the spathe.

THE DRAWING:
The boundaries of inflorescence were marked out on the page, and the spathe and stem were then accurately drawn. The 'clock-face' method was used to ascertain the complex arrangement of angles present in the sepals and petals. Finally, details in the anthers were included.

The drawing was lifted with a kneaded eraser to lighten the image in preparation for the watercolour.

NB The 'life-size' drawing opposite, has been turned through 90°

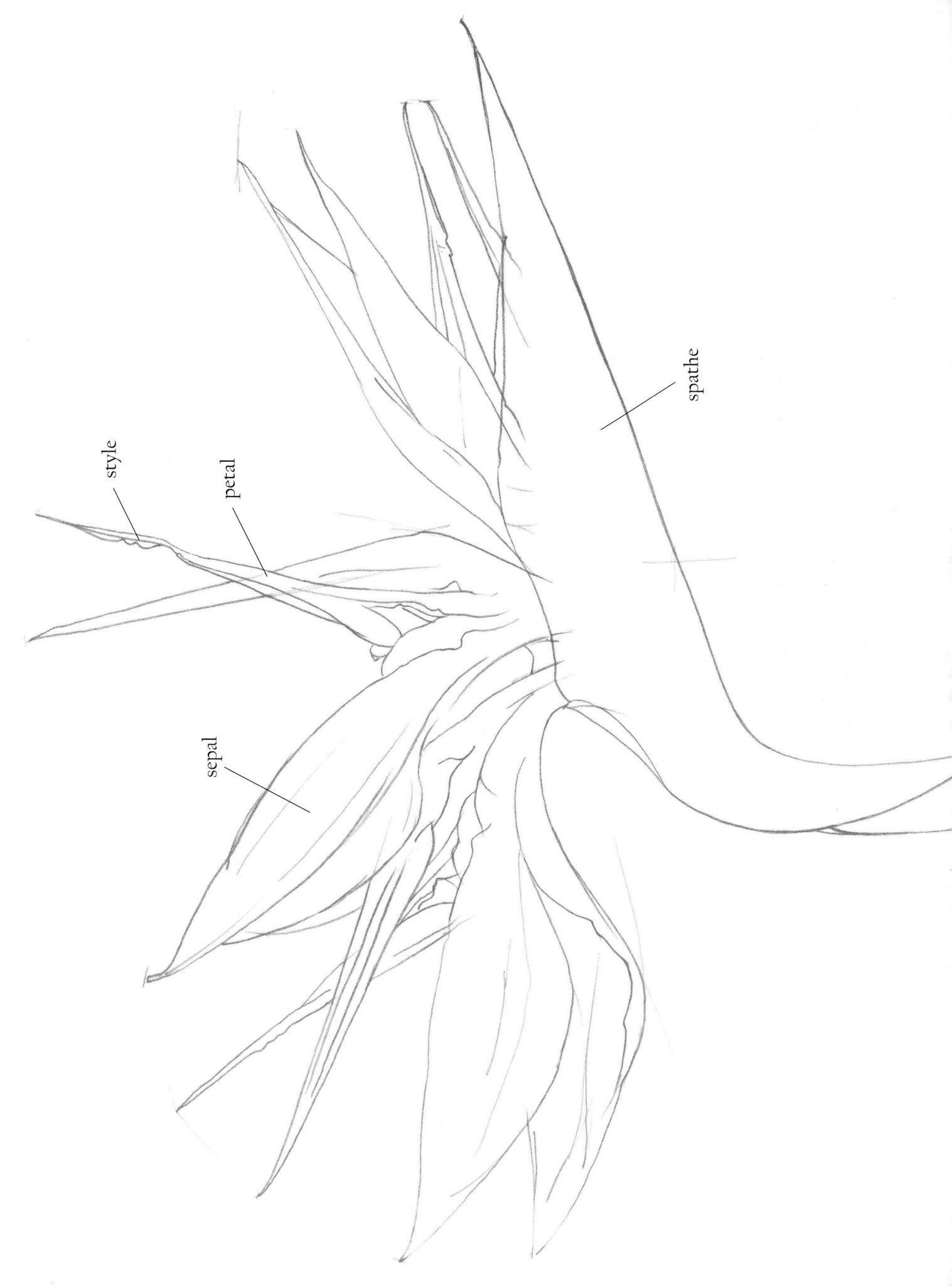

1. The petals and sepals: the first layers of blue and some shading

The basic hue of the blue petals was a mix of French ultramarine and neutral tint. The newer petals (closer to the point of the spathe) appear pale as they emerge. The colour becomes richer, and then darker as they age. The paler tints were made from a dilution of this basic hue, and the deeper tints contained the addition of a little more neutral tint. These were overlaid to intensify the colour difference in the far left petal. Some shade was applied to the base of the sepals and along the top of the spathe, using neutral tint. Some of the rose colour was also indicated, using a mixture of permanent rose and neutral tint. The paint was applied, to damp paper, using a Nº5 brush. This was blended and graded to the highlights.

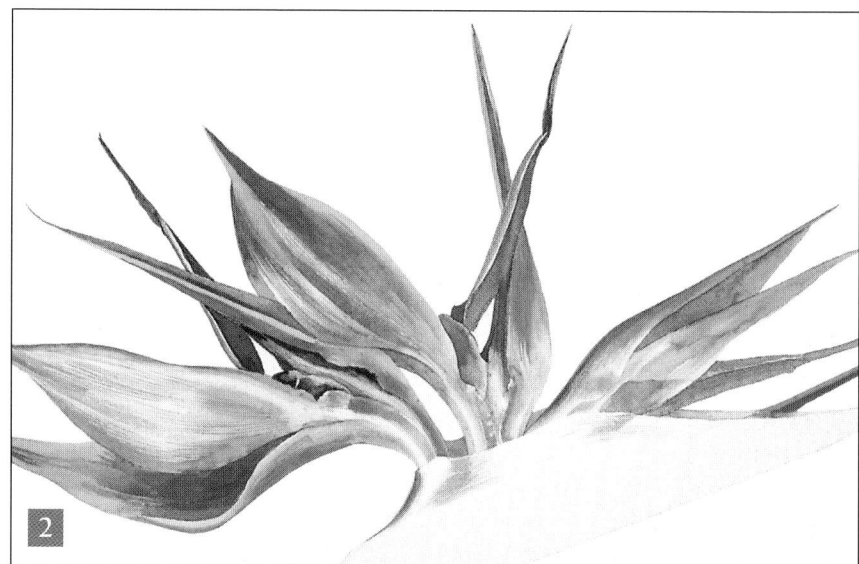

2. The styles and sepals: the layers of pale brown and orange

The styles were a mixture of raw umber and French ultramarine, with a little neutral tint added for shade. This was applied as a wash, which provides the foundation for further detail. Each one was painted onto dry paper using a Nº3 brush. The basic hue of the sepals was made from a mixture of cadmium yellow and cadmium red, with the addition of neutral tint for the shades. When opened, they appear as a range of rich mid-orange hues. The small, emerging sepal, on the far right, was painted in a rich warm orange. The first paint layers on the fully emerged sepals are biased slightly towards yellow, providing a base for a range of oranges. Using a Nº5 brush, onto damp paper, the pure hues were blended with the shaded hues. The colour was graded into the highlights, which were not painted at this stage.

3. The spathe: the first layers of pink

The dull green spathe had an under tone of dull pink. This was mixed from permanent rose and neutral tint, with a touch of cadmium yellow. This was applied with a Nº6 brush, on to dry paper, using a flat wash, which was blended into some sweeping dry brush. At this stage, the lightest parts of the spathe were not painted.

4. The styles and petals: the last layers of detail, shade and colour

The texture of the styles was defined using the pointed dry brush technique, with a Nº1 brush on dry paper, with the basic colour mixture used in stage 2. The blue petals were overlaid with the basic blue mixture used in stage 1, with a touch of Winsor violet added to this. The same brush techniques as in stage 1 were used, but this time onto dry paper.

5. The sepals: the last layers of rich deep orange

The colour of the sepals was enriched with subtler variations of warm hot orange blended with cooler yellowish orange. In addition, the shaded areas were deepened. This was applied onto dry paper with a Nº5 brush. The washes were blended, as each sepal was painted individually, working across the picture from left to right. The lightest areas showed some sheen and texture, which was defined with a sweeping dry brush. The shading at the base of each sepal and petal was also deepened, using the same techniques as in stage 1, but onto dry paper.

6. The spathe: first layers of green

The dull green of the spathe was made with French ultramarine, cadmium lemon and neutral tint. This was painted over the pink base, onto dry paper, using a Nº6 brush. The colour was laid in a flat wash, which was blended into some sweeping dry brush, which is particularly evident on the light tone areas.

7. The spathe and stem: the final layers of pink and green

The pink used in stage 3 was applied again to deepen the hue on the edge of the spathe. More neutral tint was added to the basic pink mixture for the shaded parts. The green colour, used for the spathe in stage 6, was painted onto the stem. This was applied in several layers to build the depth, using a Nº5 brush, onto dry paper. Stage 6 was repeated to build the depth of colour in the spathe. The variations in bluish or yellowish green were included to complete the full range of warm and cool colouring. The highlights on all parts were painted with a dilute wash mixture of cerulean blue and neutral tint, onto dry paper, with a Nº5 brush.

7

NB This 'life-size'
painting has been
turned through 90°

Botanical Terms

The following definitions are relevant to the plants that are drawn and painted for this book, although wider botanical meanings exist outside this context.

The following glossary consists of the botanical terms found throughout the text.

Acropetal
Development of flowers in succession, from the base upwards.

Angiosperm
Flowering plant.

Anther
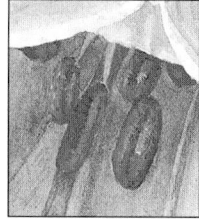
The portion of a stamen that produces pollen. (See page 75.)

Axil
The angle made between the upper part of a leaf and the stem that bears this leaf.

Bract

Leaf-like organ above which an individual flower, or inflorescence, arises. (See page 95.)

Bulb
Fleshy subterranean storage organ made of swollen scale leaves or leaf bases. Serves as an organ of perennation and vegetative propagation.

Calyx
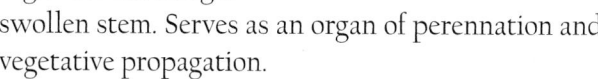
A collective term for the sepals.

Corm
Subterranean storage organ constituting a swollen stem. Serves as an organ of perennation and vegetative propagation.

Corolla
A collective term for the petals.

Cultivar
A subdivision of a species, arrived at through artificial propagation in cultivation. The term was introduced by the Royal Horticultural Society, in 1964, as a substitute for the word 'variety'.

Family
The division of botanical classification between an order and a genus, comprising similar genera. The names of botanical families usually end in –aceae.

Filament
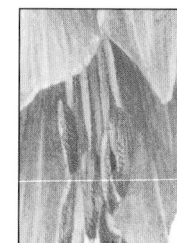
The stalk of the stamen that supports the anther. (See page 95.)

Floret
A single, small flower that forms part of a flower head.

Genus
A taxonomic rank that contains related species. Collections of similar genera are grouped together in a family.

Hybrid
A plant that is the offspring of two genetically different parents.

Inflorescence
A flowering shoot that bears more than one flower.

Lanceolate
Tapering to a point at the apex, being proportionately longer in length than width.

Midrib

The largest leaf vein running longitudinally through the centre of the leaf. (See page 111.)

Pedicel
The stalk of an individual flower that forms part of an inflorescence.

Perianth
The outer part of a flower including the calyx and the corolla or, when they are not distinct, the tepals.

Petal
Collectively forming the corolla.

Petaloid
Looking like a petal.

Petiole
The stalk of a leaf that joins it to a stem.

Pistil
A general term to describe the ovary, style and stigma, together forming the female organ of a flower.

Pollen
The mass of male microspores, formed by the anthers, usually a fine dust.

Raceme
An inflorescence with a single axis bearing separate flowers attached by stalks.

Rhizome
A root-like stem growing in prostrate fashion, producing both roots and shoots. Usually grows underground, or partially underground, acting as an agent of vegetative propogation and frequently as a storage organ in perennial plants.

Sepal
One part of the calyx, usually green.

Spadix
An inflorescence with flowers borne on a central fleshy column. Usually enclosed in a spathe (see page 118).

Spathe
A bract that envelops a spadix.

Species
The fundamental unit of classification of plants. The *specific epithet* forms the second half of the scientific name (cf genus).

Stamen
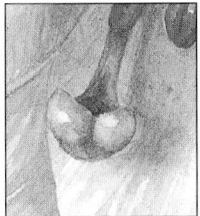
The pollen-bearing male organ of a flowering plant. Consists of a filament and anther.

Stigma
The surface area of a style that receives pollen. Usually found at the extremity of the style. (See page 75.)

Stipule
A small leaf-like outgrowth found at the foot of a petiole.

Style
The extension of an ovary that supports the stigma.

Taxonomy
The science of classifying biological life forms.

Tepal
An individual part of the perianth where there is no distinct calyx and corolla (e.g. tulip, lily etc.).

Venation

The arrangement of veins in a petal or leaf. (See page 103.)

Whorl
A ring of petals, leaves etc. arranged around a stem at a common level.

Selected bibliography

The following books are recommended as sources of further information for the Flower Painter.

BOTANY
Plant structure and taxonomy.

CAPON, Brian
Botany for Gardeners:
An Introduction and Guide
Batsford, London, 1998

JOHNSON, Arthur T.; and
SMITH, H.A.
Plant Names Simplified
Landesmans Bookshop Ltd.,
Herefordshire, 1946

RAVEN, Peter H.; EVERT, Ray F.;
EICHHORN, Susan E.,
Biology of Plants
W.H. Freeman & Co., 6th edn.,
New York, 1998

STEARN, William T.
Botanical Latin
David & Charles, 4th edn.,
Newton Abbot & London, 1995

HORTICULTURE
Choosing, finding, and growing plants.

BRICKELL, Christopher
The Royal Horticultural Society
A-Z Encyclopedia of Garden Plants
Dorling Kindersley Plc., London, 1996

GREENWOOD, Pippa
New Flower Gardener
Dorling Kindersley Plc., London, 1998

HILLIER, Malcom
Container Gardening
Through the Year
Dorling Kindersley Plc., London, 1998

RAVEN, Sarah
The Cutting Garden
Frances Lincoln, London, 1996

Royal Horticultural Society
RHS Plant Finder
Dorling Kindersley Plc., London,
Annual (June)

SEARCH, Gay
Gardening Without a Garden
Dorling Kindersley Plc., London, 1997

HISTORY
Naturalistic Flower Painting and Botanical Illustration.

BLUNT. Wilfred & STEARN, W.T.
The Art of Botanical Illustration
(2nd edn)
Antique Collectors Club, Suffolk, in
association with the Royal Botanic
Gardens, Kew, 1994

ELLIOTT, Brent
Treasures of the Royal
Horticultural Society
Herbert Press, in association with
the Royal Horticultural Society,
London 1994

HULTON, P.& SMITH, L.
Flowers in Art from East and West
British Museum Publications,
London 1979

PINAULT, Madeleine
Painter as Naturalist:
From Dürer to Redouté
Abbeville Press, New York, 1991

MALLARY, Peter & Frances
A Redouté Treasury,
468 Watercolours from Les
Liliacées of Pierre-Joseph Redouté
J. M. Dent & Sons Ltd,
London & Melbourne 1986
American edition published by
The Vendome Press, New York 1986

SCRACE, David
Flower Drawings
Cambridge University Press, 1997

SHERWOOD, Shirley
Contemporary Botanical Artists
Weidenfeld & Nicolson,
in association with Royal Botanic
Gardens, Kew, London 1997

SHERWOOD, Shirley
A Passion for plants:
Contemporary Botanical
Masterworks
Cassells, London 2001

TONGIORGI TOMASI, Lucia;
CHEN, Lisa (Translator);
LAMBERT MELLON, Rachel
An Oak Spring Flora:
Flower Illustration from
the Fifteenth Century
to the Present Time:
A Selection of Rare Books,
Manuscripts, and Works of Art
Yale University Press, 1997

WHITE, James, J.
Catalogue of International
Exhibition of Botanical Art
and Illustration
Hunt Institute for Botanical
Documentation, Carnegie Mellon
University, Pittsburg,
Pensylvania, USA, 1964 onwards
(currently 9 issued)

THEORY
For painters, illustrators, and designers.

The methods for naturalistic flower painting owe much to the definitive experiments published by J. Itten.

ITTEN, Johannes
The Art of Colour
John Wiley Inc., New York 1974

ITTEN, Johannes
The Elements of Colour
John Wiley Inc., New York 1970

Suppliers directory

STUDIO EQUIPMENT, MATERIALS, AND PAPER

The following art centres stock a comprehensive range of supplies. All have catalogues available and worldwide mail order.

ATLANTIS EUROPEAN LTD.
ART SUPPLIERS
7-9 Plummers Row
London E1 1EQ
Tel 020 7377 8855   Fax 020 7377 8850

FALKINER FINE PAPERS
76 Southampton Row
London WC1B 4AR
Tel 020 7831 1151   Fax 020 7430 1248
For paper and sketchbooks only.

JOHN JONES ART CENTRE LTD
Stroud Green Road
Finsbury Park
London N4 3JG
Tel 020 7281 5439   Fax 020 7281 5956
Website www.johnjones.co.uk
email info@johnjones.co.uk

LONDON GRAPHICS CENTRE
16-18 Shelton Street
London WC2H 9JJ
Tel 020 7240 0095   Fax 020 7831 1544
Website www.londongraphics.co.uk
email mailorder@londongraphics.co.uk

T.N. LAWRENCE AND SON LTD
117-119 Clerkenwell Road
London EC1R 5BY
Tel 020 7242 3534
For mail order:
Tel 01273 260260   Fax 01273 260270
email artbox@lawrence.co.uk
Website www.lawrence.co.uk
Branches also in Cornwall and Sussex.

MANUFACTURERS

Contact the manufacturers below to find your nearest supplier.

DALER ROWNEY
P.O. Box 10
Bracknell
Berkshire R612 8ST
England
Tel 01344 424 621   Fax 01344 860 746
email webmaster@daler-rowney.com
Website www.daler-rowney.com
For all Daler Rowney products.

BUTTENPAPIERFABRIK
HAHNEMUHLE
Postfach 4
D-3354 Dassel
Germany
Tel 49 5561 7910   Fax 49 5561 791377
www.s-und-s.de
For Hahnemuhle paper

ST. CUTHBERTS MILL
Wells
Somerset BA5 1AG
England
Tel 01749 672015   Fax 01749 678844
Website www.inveresk.co.uk
For Saunders Waterford paper.

SCHOELLERSHAMMER PAPER
Heinr. Aug. Scholler Sohne
GMBH & Co. KG
Postfach 101946
D-5160 Duren
Germany
Tel 49 2421 5570   Fax 49 2421 557 110
For Schoellershammer paper.

TWINROCKER HANDMADE PAPER
P.O. Box 413
Brookston
IN 47923
USA
Toll Free 1-800-757-TWIN
Fax (317) 563-TWIN
email twinrock@mail.com
Website www.twinrocker.com
For handmade paper Hot-Pressed paper, made to order. Worldwide mail order via website/email.

WINSOR & NEWTON
Whitefriars Avenue
Wealdstone
Harrow
Middlesex HA3 5RH
England
Tel 020 8427 4343   Fax 020 8863 7177
Website www.winsornewton.com
For all Winsor and Newton products.

LIGHTING AND OTHER EQUIPMENT

Most major art stores stock angle-poise lamps and daylight bulbs.

CLE DESIGN LTD.
Conservation Lighting and Equipment
69-71 Haydons Road
Wimbledon
London SW19 1HQ
England
Tel 020 8540 5772   Fax 020 8543 4055
email admin@cle-design.com
Website www.cle-design.com
Stockists for the Phillips TLD95 full spectrum tube light, Tungsten Daylight Bulbs, and superior quality angle-poise task lights. Catalogue available and worldwide mail order.

TWO WESTS & ELLIOTT
Tel 01246 451077   Fax 01246 260115
email sales@twowest.co.uk
For Dewpoint Cabinet (see Chapter3). Catalogue available and worldwide mail order.

Index